Research and Evaluation in the Human Services

Research and Evaluation in the Human Services

JOHN R. SCHUERMAN

THE FREE PRESS
A Division of Macmillan, Inc.
NEW YORK

Collier Macmillan Publishers
LONDON

The Free Press
A Division of Macmillan, Inc.
866 Third Avenue, New York, N. Y. 10022

Collier Macmillan Canada, Inc.

Printed in the United States of America

printing number

1 2 3 4 5 6 7 8 9 10

Library of Congress Cataloging in Publication Data

Schuerman, John R.
Research and evaluation in the human services.

Includes bibliographies and index.
1. Social service—Research. 2. Social Service—
Evaluation. I. Title.
HV11.S3823   1983   361.3'072   82-48475
ISBN 0-02-928080-X

To Mildred and Lawrence

Contents

Preface

This book is designed for undergraduate and beginning graduate students in social work and other human service professions. Its aim is to prepare professionals who will continue to develop their own personal systems of practice throughout their careers.

The book focuses on the development of practice through the systematic generation of information. The first objective is to encourage an orientation to practice that is empirically based. The second objective is the development of basic skills in the collection and interpretation of data. I stress those skills useful for evaluating and enhancing one's own practice. In addition, I hope that the book will help students read and interpret research reports.

The processes of evaluation are stressed in this book. It is particularly important to learn how to specify the objectives of intervention and the intervention procedures. I also explore the close connection between intervention and research activities.

Part I is an introduction to the place of research in practice and to basic concepts in social research. Part II is organized around types of questions that arise in practice: evaluation of work with individuals, evaluation of programs, understanding of people and their problems, and understanding the processes of intervention. Part III is a more extended treatment of various aspects of research: design, measurement, data collection, and data analysis.

The initial conception of this book was developed with my colleague Donald W. Beless. I am indebted to him for thinking through with me the structure and content and for his careful reading of several drafts. Students in Don's introductory research courses at the School of Social Service Administration of the University of Chicago used part of this book in draft form and contributed to its development.

I also appreciate thoughtful suggestions on parts of the manuscript by Dennis Klaser, Jeanne Marsh, Elsie Pinkston, Charlotte Schuerman, Matsujiro Shibano, Karen Teigiser, and Lynn Videka-Sherman.

I would like to thank SPSS, Inc., Chicago, IL for permission to cite its proprietary computer software in Chapter 12. The figures in this book were produced with the Tell-A-Graf graphics system, a product of Integrated Software Systems Corporation (ISSCO).

Finally, I appreciate the tolerance and support of my family, Charlotte, Gabrielle, and Matthew, during the course of this project.

Part 1

Introduction

1

The Development of Human Services Practice

Professionals in the human services are faced with human problems that require action. Because these are complicated human situations, it is often not immediately clear what should be done. But action must be taken. Sometimes action is taken immediately, seemingly without thinking. Other times, careful deliberation precedes the doing.

What are the sources of professional action? What are the reasons a professional does what he does when faced with a particular problem? Although the reasons are often complicated and interwoven, some of the sources of professional action can be listed:

1. *Values*. The precepts that provide the motivation for our work, the framework for our activities and the boundaries for our appropriate behavior as professionals. Values have roots in our culture, in the history of our profession, and in our own unique experience.
2. *Intuition*. Knowing seemingly without thinking what is right to do. This faculty is poorly understood. Good professionals

3

seem to have good intuition to begin with and to develop it further through experience.

3. *Knowledge*. Organized information of many kinds affecting professional action. We will have much more to say about knowledge in the next few pages.

4. *Skill*. Facility in effective action. Skill usually comes with practice.

Other ways of categorizing the sources of professional action could be developed. This is not the place for a detailed examination of why practitioners act as they do when faced with a particular problem; rather, in this book we focus on one of the above sources of action, knowledge. We will be concerned with several types of knowledge.

Knowledge

The professional worker makes use of knowledge in several areas:

1. Knowledge about the particular case or situation, that is, knowledge about what the problem is and its background.
2. Knowledge about similar cases or situations.
3. Knowledge about human behavior and development, about human interaction, social structure, and other social phenomena.
4. Knowledge about what has worked in the past in similar situations.
5. Knowledge of oneself, one's strengths and weaknesses, and particularly knowledge about those actions which seem to be successful when one does them.

Knowledge comes from our experience and that of those around us. Since some experiences teach us more than others, we may be quite certain of particular parts of our knowledge and feel rather shaky elsewhere. And, of course, people differ in the extent of confidence they have about various pieces of knowledge.

Some ways of developing knowledge are more likely than others to produce statements with a high degree of confidence, and it is possible to arrange our experiences to this end. This book is about systematic ways of developing knowledge in the human services. We call such approaches *research*.

Research

As stated, most of this book is about systematic procedures that can be used to develop knowledge. At this point we want to mention some particularly important ideas.

First, research always begins with one or more questions or hypotheses. Questions ask about the true state of affairs, while hypotheses are statements about how things might be.

Examples of research questions are:

1. What is the relationship between economic deprivation and delinquent behavior?
2. What are the factors that lead to riots in prisons?
3. What are the stresses experienced by new immigrants in this country?

Examples of hypotheses are:

1. Treatment which is structured is generally more effective than treatment which is not structured.
2. Families which are extremely close or extremely distant emotionally are more likely to produce children with psychological disturbances than families that are not so extreme.
3. The provision of day care services, job training programs, and counseling reduces the number of persons dependent on public assistance.

Sometimes questions can be turned into hypotheses. For example, the first question above could be phrased as an hypothesis: Persons who are economically deprived are more likely to engage in delinquent behavior than those who are not.

Other questions, however, are less specific than hypotheses, as for example, questions two and three. Usually questions and hypotheses are general in nature. That is, instead of referring to a specific individual or situation, they concern a number of individuals or a set of situations. After establishing questions or hypotheses the researcher attempts to answer the questions or test the hypotheses to determine whether or not the latter are true.

To answer questions or test hypotheses the researcher must gather data. Data consist of observations or measurements designed to determine what the state of affairs is in a number of specific situations. It is here that it is most important to be systematic. We want to be assured that the observations and measurements are accurate. Beyond that, one of the fundamental requirements of data is that they be replicable; it should be possible for another researcher to make similar observations in similar circumstances for the sake of comparison. This can be done only if the first researcher collects his data systematically and reports his procedures fully.

Therefore, the researcher should follow carefully specified procedures. This is not to say that research should be inflexible. On the contrary, a good researcher responds to insights developed along the way and may shift data collection procedures, change the data being collected, or even change the question being asked. But such changes should occur consciously and the research should continue to proceed systematically.

We can get a better idea of what we mean by research by considering different kinds of research and some of the ways it is carried out. There are a number of different ways of categorizing research. We will consider three of them.

KINDS OF QUESTIONS

First, one can classify research in terms of the kinds of questions being asked. For the professional practitioner, there are three types of questions that are of importance:

1. Does what I am doing work? Or to be more specific, what works under what circumstances to produce what outcomes? These questions come under the heading of *evaluation*.
2. What is the nature of the problems I face? What are their sources and dynamics? What perpetuates them?
3. What is the nature of the individuals, families, organizations, or communities with which I am working? For example, what are the dynamics of human behavior, organizational behavior, communities, or societies?

Evaluation. Evaluation gets at the core of professional practice. Obviously the most critical thing to ask about practice activities is whether or not they are effective. In an applied profession, the ultimate problem is finding out what works under what circumstances. Usually this is put in terms of whether desired changes occur as a result of professional action. Sometimes we evaluate our work with a particular case such as that of an individual, family, community, or other social entity. At other times we evaluate the impact of a social program on a group of clients.

Recent years have seen a dramatic increase in interest in evaluation. This phenomenon dates from the large scale social programs of the 1960s and reflects a need to determine whether the programs had the desired impact. Recently, the meaning of evaluation has been enlarged. Originally it meant simply determining whether or not some activity was successful. Now the term is used more broadly, sometimes seeming to include all research which might be applied in solving practical problems. In this book, the term will have a somewhat more limited meaning. By evaluation we mean descriptions of professional activities, investigations of the effects of professional activities, experimentation on new forms of intervention, and research designed to develop more effective interventions.

Because evaluation is so important in the development of a profession, it is a major concern in this book.

Research on the nature of problems. Obviously it is important that practitioners have some understanding of the problems they face. Thus much research is directed to this goal. Included here is research on how problems develop, their dynamics, and the factors contributing to their continuation or alleviation. Examples of this are research on the sources of delinquent behavior, on the relationship between family interaction and the continuation of psychiatric illness, and the reasons for dependency and neglect of children.

Research on the Nature of Individuals, Families, Organizations, and Communities. Included here is research on normal human growth and development, problem solving, social structure, family dynamics, political processes, and so forth. For example we might do research on the so called normal stresses experienced by new mothers, the processes by which committees work, or the reasons for shifts in political sentiments. Often research in this category (and the previous one as well) is carried out by individuals from academic social science disciplines such as sociology, psychology, and political science. It is possible, however, for professionals in applied fields also to pursue these issues.

METHOD OF ANSWERING QUESTIONS

A second way of categorizing research has to do with the method used for answering the question. Some research gathers information on groups of individuals or groups of some other entities like communities, states, and so forth. We will call this *group research*. The term *nomothetic research* is also used. Another kind of research gathers data on only one or a small number of cases at once. We will call such research *single case research*. The term *ideographic research* is also used for this type of study.

Group research is often aimed at developing general knowledge of some kind, that is, knowledge that applies to many different situations or that concerns relatively large groups of people. Group research is also used to evaluate whole service programs. By its nature, single case research produces information on only a few specific individuals or situations at one time. However, general knowledge is advanced through single case research when the particular study is one of a series concerning the same general problem. Single case research is often used to evaluate highly specific intervention techniques. In the chapters that follow we will develop a number of subcategories of both group and single case research.

KINDS OF CONCLUSIONS

The third way of categorizing research concerns the kinds of conclusions we can draw from the data. Some data allow us merely to describe a group of people, to say what their characteristics are. We will call such research *descriptive*. For example, we might want to describe the people who live in a particular community and to say what kinds of problems they are experiencing. A second kind of data allows us to explore the relationships or associations among characteristics. Such research is called *correlational*. For example, we might want to know whether economic deprivation is related to delinquency. Finally, a third kind of research called *causal research* tries to explain why things happen. For example, we might want to know whether a particular intervention technique is effective, that is, whether it causes improvement, or we might want to establish that economic deprivation causes delinquency.

BASIC AND APPLIED RESEARCH

Before leaving our discussion of various ways of categorizing research, we want to make some comments on another distinction that is often made, that between applied and basic research. Basic research means research designed to develop theory, while applied research means those activities designed to provide information that can be utilized for some end. In practice, most applied research has at least some implications for the development of theory. At the same time, basic research very often has led to important applications.

Objectives of this Book

This book is oriented to practice: to improving practice generally and to enabling individual practitioners to enhance their own practice. Practice is developed and improved through the increased use of systematic knowledge. At the same time it is recognized that most readers of this book will not devote their careers to research, although I hope some will. I hope to provide readers with those tools necessary to understand published reports of research studies. Beyond that, I hope to provide skills and attitudes useful for applying research ideas in such a way that one's own practice can be improved. For the direct service practitioner, I believe that the techniques of single case study are particularly applicable. The emphasis, therefore, is on understanding group research and on applying single case methods. The focus is upon developing skills that may be applied in day to day practice. I believe one's practice will be enhanced through systematically assessing the outcomes of one's own work in specific situations.

In addition, I hope that this book will have another impact. I believe that there is an important parallel between the processes of research and the processes of good practice. Practice is more effective if it is systematic. The core of systematic practice is the clear specification of objectives and of the proposed means for achieving them. I hope these ideas, central to this book, and the ways of thinking presented here will be of direct use for professionals in the development of their own practice.

Summary

This chapter began by placing knowledge in the context of other influences on professional activity. Research is one of the ways by which we develop knowledge, a systematic way that leads to knowledge in which we can be relatively confident.

Any research attempts to answer one or more questions or to test one or more hypotheses. Three ways of categorizing research were considered: the kinds of questions posed, the method used to answer the questions, and the kinds of conclusions that can be reached.

2

The Processes of Research

In this chapter we provide an overview of the processes of research. As we do this, a number of basic ideas will be introduced, ideas which will come up frequently in the rest of the book. The processes will be described as if they occur in discrete phases in the course of a research project. In fact, in real life this rarely happens. Rather, phases merge into each other and more than one of the processes may occur at the same time.

We will use as an example a hypothetical study comparing highly structured intervention with intervention that is not so highly structured. The location for our study is a family service agency and the study is limited to cases of parent-child conflict.

Defining the Problem

As indicated in Chapter 1, research always begins with one or more questions or hypotheses. Questions may ask: What is the state of affairs? How are things related to each other? or What happens if such and such occurs? Hypotheses are statements about what we think the state of affairs is. Here our hypothesis might be that highly structured intervention is more effective than less structured intervention. The formulation of the questions or hypotheses serves as the basis for the activities that make up the rest of the research project.

That seems simple enough, but there are often great difficulties encountered in defining the research problem. Since the initial question or statement should suggest what needs to be done in order to proceed, not all questions or hypotheses can be used as the basis of a research effort.

The first formulation of a research question often is too global; that is, it asks a question much too big to be answered in a single research project or a question which would require vast quantities of data to answer. Such a question might be: What are the causes of mental illness?

To be useful this would have to be broken down, or narrowed, and only small parts of the original question kept. One might focus on only one form of mental illness (for example, a particular type of schizophrenia) and one set of possible causes (such as early childhood experiences).

The second major flaw in the initial formulation of a question is that it often is too vague to serve as a guide to research. This is usually because the words employed have multiple or unclear meanings. Thus the question often has to be reformulated so that the words used are clear and precise in meaning. In our example, it is important to clearly define what is meant by structured and effective.

Research questions contain verbal abstractions called *concepts*. The notions of structured intervention and effective intervention are examples of this. Since concepts are so important to research and theory, we need to talk about them.

CONCEPTS

Through our senses, we are continually receiving information about the world. The sensations we receive make impressions on our minds which we call *percepts* or *perceptions*. Every day we experience an enormous variety of percepts. This bombardment of raw experience would be totally bewildering were it not for the fact that the mind is able to organize its perceptions into a much smaller number of categories. A concept is a category of perceptions or experiences. It can also be thought of as a grouping of objects or events in the world. Further, the mind establishes relationships among the categories or concepts.

We label concepts with words and this allows us to think about them and communicate them to other people. We call the process of categorizing and labeling *conceptualization.* Scientists have developed this process to a high art. The advance of science continually requires new concepts, new ways of categorizing objects and events that have been seen before, and new categories for objects and events never seen before.

Different observers of the same scene often have different perceptions of what they see. Even if two people have similar perceptions, they may have different conceptions; that is, they may put their perceptions into different categories. Differences in perception and conceptualization are particularly common when dealing with social phenomena, because social events are so complicated.

Suppose we observe a third grade classroom in which one of the boys repeatedly strikes other children. Perceptions of this situation might well differ, in that an observer might or might not take note of what the boy was hitting with, how he was hitting, whom he was hitting (both boys and girls or one or the other) as well as what else was going on in the classroom. Even if two people had similar perceptions, their conceptions might differ, one labeling the behavior as aggressive, the other as playful.

We have talked about concepts as categories of perceptions or observable phenomena. Sometimes concepts are combined into higher order concepts (some authors call these *constructs*). In the situation above, aggressive behavior might be included in a higher order concept like release of libidinal impulse or operant behavior. There is, therefore, a hierarchy of concepts, increasing in abstractness as one rises in the hierarchy. More abstract concepts are very useful in developing theory, in bringing seemingly diverse phenomena together into one explanatory framework.

Since we can have lots of different concepts for the same perceptions (that is, we can think about things in many different ways) the question naturally arises as to how one chooses among the various possibilities. As we have developed the idea here, there are no such things as right or wrong concepts, since they are simply categories constructed by the mind. One can, however, be right or wrong about the relationships among concepts.

The criterion we prefer for the selection of concepts is usefulness. Concepts may not be right or wrong, but they do differ in usefulness. There are two aspects of this that are important. First of all, concepts must be useful for theorizing. They ought to bring together lower level concepts and worldly phenomena in ways that suggest possible connections or relationships. They ought to serve the imagination so that new ways of thinking about the world emerge. Second, concepts must be useful for research. Since research is concerned with gathering information to help answer some question, we must have concepts that point to particular pieces of information, that suggest what data should be gathered and how. The two aspects of usefulness are sometimes in conflict; one might have a very imaginative concept that leads to complex and ingenious theorizing but which is hard to define in terms of observable phenomena. An example might be the concept of ego strength. On the other hand, one might have a very concrete concept which is too mundane to serve theoretical purposes. This conflict between usefulness and concreteness has led to much debate.

Research questions contain more or less abstract concepts, like structured intervention and parent-child conflict. The elaboration of a research question must lead to observable phenomena. In a way, the process of developing high order concepts must be reversed. Higher level concepts must be defined in terms of lower level concepts until we reach the point at which we have low order concepts defined in terms of observable phenomena: percepts.

Operational concepts are those that have been defined in terms of observable phenomena. In our example we would operationalize the concept of structured intervention by specifying its characteristics, enabling us to decide whether it had been used in particular cases. The criteria might be:

1. An established time limit for service.
2. Specific and concrete goals, agreed upon by the worker and client, for changes in behavior.
3. A clear understanding of specific and concrete steps to be taken by clients and worker in each phase of their work together.

The concept of parent-child conflict might be determined by having the clients and/or worker rate the level of conflict, or the number of times the parent and child get into arguments might be counted.

In this book we will make frequent use of the idea of a *variable*. A variable is a characteristic that different people or social systems have in different quantities. A variable may also be a characteristic that a particular person has in different amounts at different points in time. For example, level of conflict is a variable. We will also use the term for a way of categorizing people. Race, psychiatric diagnosis, and whether or not a family received structured intervention are variables. The term will also be used to denote the occurrence or nonoccurrence of an event, for example, the occurrence or nonoccurrence of an argument or of delinquent behavior. Social research may be thought of as an effort to explain or predict the occurrence of events or the variations in characteristics among people or social systems.

So we begin the research endeavor with relatively broad kinds of questions and proceed to narrow these questions down to more specific issues. Eventually we must specify the question in terms of operationalized concepts, observable things. The process involves the development of definitions of concepts.

DEFINITIONS

Definitions used in the social sciences specify concepts by describing the attributes of their components. The basic criterion for a good definition is whether or not it is clear that something falls in the category labeled by the concept. If we have a definition for the concept of chair, it must be such that it is clear whether or not an object is to be thought of as a chair. The definition should clearly include all those objects we want to include and clearly exclude all other objects. A definition of a chair as something on which persons sit would be relatively unambiguous but would not capture the usual meaning of the word. It would include a number of objects we would want to leave out (benchs or couches) and might exclude some objects we want to include (chairs on which no one had ever seen anybody sitting). The definition should be such that there will be a minimum of argument about whether something is to be included. For example, a definition of a chair as a comfortable place to sit would invite disagreement about whether a particular sitting place was comfortable.

Definitions never perfectly meet the requirements set forth above. The best definition I can come up with for chair is a seat for one person that is usually moveable, typically having four legs and a back and sometimes arms.[1]

There are two kinds of operational concepts that we define in research: variables and the categories that make up some variables. A variable definition specifies those characteristics that are to be taken into account in determining the category or value of an individual on that variable. For example, a definition of gender would specify those characteristics of people or animals that are to be considered in determining whether an individual is male or female. Similarly, a definition of change in level of conflict would specify those things in the interaction of parents and children that are to be considered in determining change, such as number of arguments. Concepts such as change in level of conflict do not have discrete categories so we need to know what to look at in order to determine where on the variable the person or family falls, whether high or low and how high or low. The definition of a category specifies those characteristics that must be present for us to put an object or person into that category. For example, the definition of structured intervention must tell us the characteristics intervention must have to be categorized as structured.

Finally, for variable concepts we need some kind of specification as to the class of individuals or objects to which the definition applies. Often this is obvious (it makes no sense to apply gender to a profession—professions are neither male nor female) but sometimes it is not (should extent of rehabilitation be applied to anyone who has ever had a cold or only to persons with severe chronic medical conditions?). In our example, changes in level of conflict might apply only to families which have experienced parent-child conflicts.

THEORY

A theory is a collection of concepts together with their definitions and a series of statements about relationships among those concepts. Theories also contain data claims, that is, assertions that such and such data support statements about relationships among concepts. For example, a theory of schizophrenia might claim that a particular series of studies supports the idea that family communication patterns are related to the development of this illness. Within a particular theory the statements of relationships have varying degrees of proof; thus one can be more confident of some than of others. Research helps in the development of theory by providing evidence for or against relationships among concepts.

Theories are always about particular parts of the world. Even within a highly developed science like physics there is (so far) no unified theory that encompasses everything with which the science is concerned. In the social sciences, although there have been attempts at grand theories, explaining all aspects of human behavior, the most successful theories are those that are more restricted and concern themselves with relatively small sets of phenomena.

One of the most important aspects of theorizing is to establish the boundaries of the theory, to creatively define the set of phenomena of interest. New theories are often successful because they are concerned with a slightly different category of events, suggesting a new point of view. Conflicts between theories in the same discipline often revolve around their attempts to account for different aspects of reality. A classic example of this in the social sciences is the conflict between psychoanalytic and behavioral theories. Behavioral theories are primarily concerned with how behavior develops and is changed while psychoanalytic theory is concerned with internal psychological conflicts and how those conflicts can be resolved. Clashes between such theories can rarely be resolved since the same set of data cannot be used to test both theories. Practitioners must choose which theory to use on the basis of practicality and effectiveness, a choice that often is not easy.

Functions of theories. A theory organizes what we know about a particular part of reality in a coherent way so that the knowledge can be communicated and more easily learned. Usually there are a few central ideas, basic concepts, or organizing principles around which the theory is built. For example, one theory of delinquency is built around the concept of the discrepancy between one's expectations for achievement and one's opportunities for achievement.[2] When we understand the basic concepts of a theory we have gone a long way toward understanding it.

Theories tell how things are related and how they fit together, and attempt to describe the causes of certain events. Sometimes they also perform a predictive function, often advancing statements like: If certain conditions occur then such and such will happen.

Theories in practice fields give coherence to one's work and a framework for thinking about the problems one faces. They provide a way to analyze and understand specific situations. In an applied profession it is desirable to have theories that go even further and provide prescriptions. Ideally, they tell us what we should do in a situation if we want a particular outcome. Few theories in the human service professions achieve this ideal. Rather than being highly specific, they provide only broad guidelines for action.

Theories and research have a close, if sometimes tense, relationship. Theories identify important questions to be answered through research by proposing new relationships among concepts.

RELATIONSHIPS AMONG CONCEPTS

Research questions almost always concern relationships among concepts or variables. It is useful to categorize the various kinds of relationships that are involved. Sometimes a question merely asks whether two or more variables are related; this kind of question we will call *descriptive*. Another kind of question is that which asks whether one thing causes another thing (we will have more to say about causal relationships and the concept of cause later on). We will call such questions *explanatory*. Finally, it is possible to predict something without really understanding its causes, so we can ask questions about how we could predict whether or not such and such will happen and we will call such questions *predictive*.

When we investigate relationships among variables we will distinguish between *dependent* and *independent* variables. Dependent variables are the variables we are trying to explain or predict. These are also called *response* or *outcome* variables. Independent variables are variables we think cause or predict the dependent variable. Independent variables are also called *predictor* variables.

What makes for good research questions? We have already talked about the importance of questions being made up of operational concepts. Beyond that, a few other things can be said.

Certain kinds of questions should be excluded as research questions. So-called normative questions are forbidden. These are questions which ask: What should be done? or What should the situation be? Such questions involve norms or values and require us to specify what we want to happen or what the state of affairs should be. There is no way to gather data on those questions. Research cannot answer the question, Should all people have an adequate income? It is, however, often possible for research to throw light on the discussion of such matters. Although what is adequate is a normative issue, research could help determine the effects of various levels of income on people. Further, it would be possible for research to help find ways to redistribute income in our society and to determine the effects of the changes on the economy, social relations, and so forth.

The above does not imply that social research is or should be value free. The questions chosen for investigation are very much affected by the values of the researcher. Beyond that, values help to determine the propriety of certain research procedures.

Another kind of question which is usually inappropriate for research is a negative question. Such questions ask why something did not happen or why such and such is not the case. It is very difficult to answer questions like: Why is the world not flat? Why have there never been unicorns? or Why do some mental patients not get better? If one is interested in such questions it is better to rephrase them in positive ways: Why is the world spherical? or What are the conditions under which mental patients get better?

As stated earlier, the final determination of whether a research question is a good one depends upon the extent to which it provides a basis and guide for the research process. A research question should point to certain data to be gathered and suggest from whom the data should be gathered. In a way, this final test of adequacy cannot be evaluated until the research is over.

It often happens that research questions shift after the project has begun, sometimes after much of the data have been collected.

This may be because difficulties have been encountered or more interesting questions have come up in the course of the research. Although this frequently occurs, it does not relieve the investigator of the responsibility to be as clear and specific as possible in the initial statement of the problem. The present author is very skeptical of the all too common practice of going into a research project without clearly specified questions, justifying the activity as exploratory research. Social research is usually costly in time, money, and sometimes social relations. Such costs are not justifiable in the presence of vague questions.

QUESTIONS IN EVALUATIVE RESEARCH

As indicated in the first chapter, the statement of the research question in evaluative research would seem to be straightforward: Is such and such a procedure effective? However, the apparent simplicity rapidly disappears in the face of the reality of most evaluation efforts. There are the usual difficulties in definition of concepts, and the specification of what the procedure or program consists of and what effectiveness means. Beyond that, it is usually necessary to focus the question on one of a number of subquestions: is the program being carried out according to plan? what is it that is actually happening in it? what people with what kinds of problems are being affected in what ways and why? what is the impact of the environment on the program and vice versa? It is usually impossible for a single evaluation to address all of these questions so choices have to be made on the basis of what is likely to be the most useful information as well as what is feasible. Thus it is important that the objectives of the evaluation be clear.

One distinction that is sometimes made in evaluation work is that between *formative* and *summative* evaluation. Formative evaluation is employed during the stage in which a program is still under development or is being newly implemented. The objective of such research is the generation of information useful for shaping and revising the program. Such evaluation often focuses on what is actually being done or variations in what is done, perhaps variations resulting from different workers in the same program. Such data are then compared to (evaluated against) the original program objectives and plan, and either the plan or the actual operations are modified accordingly. Formative evaluation generally does not focus on eventual outcomes of the program.

Summative evaluation on the other hand asks the question: Does the program, as a whole, work? Such research should be undertaken only after the program has achieved some stability (sometimes an elusive objective in social programs) and after it has gone on for some time and a reasonable number of persons have completed it. To answer the question with any confidence, summative evaluation generally must be much more highly structured than formative evaluation. This is because the ultimate objective in summative research is to make causal assertions; that is, this program had this effect which would not have occurred in its absence or with another program. As we shall see later, particular kinds of research designs lead to more confidence in assertions of cause and effect relationships.

Design

The design for a research project is the plan for answering the research question. It specifies what information (data) is needed, from whom, and when it is to be gathered.

The first step is to determine which individuals, groups, or other social systems will be involved in the study. This is the *sample*, comprised of *subjects*. In our example we might select all those families who come to the agency with parent-child problems during a particular period of time. The confidence we have in our data depends on the size of the sample and how it is selected. We will discuss sampling in more detail later on.

Once the sample is determined, we must decide what information is required and when it is to be obtained. These decisions may be simple or complex. In the case of a study attempting to describe the clientele of an agency the design might be very simple: the researcher might examine a sample of agency files for a particular period of time and extract certain data from the files. The important design decisions in this case would be what period to examine, how to select the sample, and what data to extract.

On the other hand, a study that attempted to determine the relative efficacy of several approaches to intervention with different groups of clients might have a rather complex design.

Studies whose objective is the determination of causal relationships (which includes many evaluation studies) almost always require greater care in design than those that are primarily descriptive (although the latter often require fairly complex sampling plans). If I think that A causes B (for example, psychotherapy is beneficial for neurotics) you usually will be able to think of a number of other things that might have caused B (maybe the passage of time causes neurotics to get better no matter what, or maybe it isn't the psychotherapy but the attention, or the fees, or something else that causes improvement). These alternative explanations are a major concern in designing studies of cause and effect. Thus we attempt to design studies in which alternative explanations are ruled out or at least are less plausible than those under examination. We talk about this as controlling for alternative explanations. When we randomly assign some subjects to a group that receives treatment and others to a group that does not, taking measurements before and after treatment, we are attempting to control for alternative explanations. Sometimes it is possible to achieve some degree of control solely through the data analysis, but statistical control is never as satisfying as control through design. We will explore the idea of control of alternative explanations through design and data analysis more extensively later in this book.

Measurement

The process of determining or estimating the values of a variable for different individuals is called *measurement*. Although value seems to imply numbers, we will think of measurement here as having a somewhat broader meaning: the process of assigning symbols, whether numbers, letters, words, or something else, to represent values. Thus the words *male* and *female* will be thought of as values for gender and *structured* and *unstructured* as values for type of intervention.

The process of developing the procedures for measurement overlaps considerably with the process of operationalizing concepts discussed earlier. Some authors consider them to be the same thing, and indeed for some variable concepts operationalization provides the measurement (for example, determination of gender). For other variables, developing measurement procedures involves more work, as when we develop a series of questions that are to be used to measure an attitude. The assignment of values may be straightforward or complicated, determined from a single piece of information or from a number of sources.

In this book we discuss a number of measurement devices and ways of developing measures.

The Quality of Data

There are many different devices available for determining distance, ranging from sensitive, highly accurate calipers to ordinary wooden yardsticks to the odometer of a car. The data on the distance between two points provided by these devices differs considerably in accuracy or quality. We will discuss three aspects of quality that are of concern in social science measurements: discrimination, reliability, and validity.

DISCRIMINATION

Discrimination is the ability to tell one individual or object from another, the fineness of the measurement. A ruler with markings every thirty-second of an inch is more discriminating than a yardstick with markings every quarter of an inch. A measure of family economic status that merely distinguishes the poor from the nonpoor is less discriminating than one which distinguishes further by specifying levels of income in dollars.

RELIABILITY

Scientists have learned from painful experience that measurements are almost always subject to error. Measurements are estimates of real values. These estimates are usually not exactly correct. Scientists hope that the estimates provided by their measurement procedures are close enough to render the research worthwhile. Researchers have developed ways to think about error and to try to determine how much of it exists in measurement.

Usually a distinction is made between two types of error: nonsystematic or random error and systematic error or bias. Random error is associated with the idea of reliability and systematic error with validity.

The notion of random error assumes there are influences that cause our measurements to fluctuate in nonsystematic ways from the true values. A child taking a test might be distracted momentarily and thus make a mistake or might not bother to look at a problem and mark the right answer by chance. A man asked his opinion of the President might have just come from an argument with his boss and give a more negative response than he would otherwise. A question on a survey might be badly worded so that people interpret it differently and thus answer it differently, even though their attitudes might be the same. Reliability depends upon the stability of the measuring process. Would we get the same result if we were to repeat the measurement?

It might be argued that there is no such thing as random error in measurement. Random error implies that there are factors affecting the measurement for which there are no explanations. In theory, if not in practice, it should be possible to track down all of these and explain them. The examples given above all had explanations for the measurement error.

However, all of these examples are of influences on the measurement that accidentally occurred at the particular time it was taken and would not be expected to happen otherwise. They are therefore thought of as random influences. A good (reliable) measurement procedure will be relatively unaffected by such factors.

The extent to which measurements are affected by random errors varies considerably; that is, some measures tend to be more in error than others. Thus it is useful to specify the amount of random error in measurements. Actually, researchers measure the amount of a measurement that is not random error and call it the reliability of a measure. The determination of reliability depends on obtaining two or more measures of the same thing and seeing how closely they agree. If we are counting the number of arguments between a child and his parents we might have two observers watch the interaction between parents and child. Each observer would count the number of arguments and reliability would be determined by the extent of agreement between the two observers.

VALIDITY

Some books suggest that validity has to do with the extent to which we are measuring what we want to measure. We will begin with that idea and expand on it. There are a number of aspects to validity.

First of all, it is possible that a measure was constructed poorly and simply does not measure what it is supposed to. For example, a measure of problem-solving skills might test reading ability as well. While reading ability is probably related to problem-solving ability, they are not the same thing, and it would be desirable to have a test for the latter independent of the former. Similarly, changes in the rating of parent-child conflicts might reflect parental optimism rather than actual changes in the frequency of conflict.

A somewhat different aspect of validity concerns concepts made up of several components, such as the concept of social functioning. In instances such as these, we want to be sure that a measure includes all of the necessary elements. This type of validity is called *factorial validity*.

Still another aspect of validity which has been the subject of great controversy in recent years concerns the problem of subgroups of subjects responding differently to a measure, when in theory, these differences are irrelevant to the concept being measured. The most prominent case of such measures is that of intelligence or mental aptitude tests.

Some writers have argued that such tests are biased against minority groups. There appear to be two major sources of such bias. First, the understanding of items on tests may be affected by terms that have different meanings in different cultures. Thus a person raised in a culture in which certain words were not used or had different meanings would be disadvantaged in taking some tests. The other source of bias comes from differential educational opportunities for certain groups. A person from a minority group may not read as well as others merely because of poor schooling. A test of mental ability should not be sensitive to such factors. There has been much debate about cultural bias in psychological tests.

The Measurement of Validity. It is often not possible to establish conclusively whether a measure is valid. It is, however, possible to explore the question of validity. Validity depends upon the conceptualization of the variable being measured and the theory from which the concept is derived. We start by going back over the steps we went through in defining the concept and then try to think of other concept variables that should be related to our measure. The exploration of validity then proceeds by examining the relationships between the variable with which we are concerned and other variables to see if these relationships are what we expect. In our example, the variable of change in parent-child conflict should be related to other aspects of the parent-child relationship and perhaps to things like self-esteem. This type of validity checking is called *construct* validity.

In a study it is important to try to have more than one measure of major variables. For example, if we were studying ways of treating depression, we might have two measures for it, one based on a checklist of symptoms and the other based on observation of behavior. We would look at the association between these; if relatively high it would be an indication that both measures are valid. Change in parent-child conflict measured by counting arguments should be related to ratings of change made by clients and workers. This kind of validity testing is sometimes called *concurrent* validity.

In a case in which one variable follows another we call the validity being tested *predictive.* For example, we would think that scholastic ability would relate to or predict future academic achievement and might look at this association to check out the validity of a measure of the former.

The investigation of the cultural bias of measures is particularly difficult, as is evidenced by the debates on this subject. If cultural groups do not differ in their responses to measures, this would be an indication that this kind of bias is not present. If, however, differences are found, the situation is more complicated. Cultural bias is not proven by such a finding, since the cultural groups may in fact differ on the variable.

In testing concurrent validity we may have two measures that are so similar they are really two forms of the same measure. Thus we are really testing reliability. On the other hand, the testing of construct validity seems to overlap with the main job of the study, the test of the hypotheses or the answering of questions. Despite these ambiguities, the concept of validity of measurement has proven to be useful in thinking about the meaning of research data.

Although it is highly desirable to investigate the reliability and validity of at least the most important variables of a study, it is sometimes not feasible to do so. Of course, with some variables, unreliability and invalidity may not be serious threats. For example, normally it is possible to determine gender reliably and validly. Even gender may present problems, however, if first names are depended upon. Then there is the possibility of errors in the recording and handling of the data and carelessness on the part of interviewers, coders, and keypunch operators, all of which would contribute to unreliability of the measures.

In the event that it is not possible to study the reliability and validity of measures, it is still important to identify possible sources of error (both random and systematic) in the measurement procedure so as to reduce their effects.

Data Reduction and Analysis

The results of the measurement operations are, of course, the data: lists of the values of each variable for all subjects of the study. In social science research this often involves a large amount of information. Somehow in this mass of material, answers to the original questions of the study must be found. Following are the steps necessary to obtain these answers:

1. Cleaning the data. The first step is rather mundane. The objective here is to find and correct obvious errors in the data. This usually involves trying to find values or combinations of values that are impossible.
2. Reducing the data. Sometimes our data comes from a number of items all of which are supposed to measure the same thing. In this step, these items are combined to give us a single value for the variable of interest. Sometimes statistical techniques

are used to suggest ways in which items or variables might be combined usefully.
3. Investigating reliability and validity. This is done through applying the principles outlined earlier in this chapter and in chapter 11.
4. Describing the sample. It is desirable to describe the nature of the sample in terms of the main variables of the study. Here relatively simple statistical techniques are useful. We might determine how many people are in each category or at each level of a variable (this is known as a *frequency distribution*). We might also determine the mean (average) or median (the score above which not more than half the scores lie) of the values for certain variables. Finally, we might describe how much variation there is in a given variable. This is done by finding the *standard deviation, variance,* or *interquartile range* (all of which are described in Chapter 12).
5. Describing relationships. The core of the research process is finding relationships among concepts, and this requires us to look at relationships among variables. There are many different ways to measure relationships, some of which we will consider later in this book.
6. Establishing statistical control. Often we are interested in asserting a causal relationship between two things. The mere fact that they are related does not mean that they are cause and effect. Statistical control attempts to make assertions of causal connection more (or less) plausible. It does this by the introduction of control variables to the analysis. These represent other explanations for the relationship between the main variables. If a relationship between two variables remains after controlling it for other variables, we can be more confident in asserting a causal relationship.

Summary

This chapter presents an overview of the processes of research.

The first step in the planning of research is the definition of the problem. Research begins with one or more questions or hypotheses which must be specified and elaborated in order to develop ways to answer them. Questions and hypotheses contain concepts, ideas which must be carefully defined. At least some of the concepts must be operationalized, suggesting the variables of the study. Most research is concerned with uncovering relationships among variables.

Once the research problem has been defined, the design for the research must be developed. The design consists of a sampling plan and a structure for the collection of data. It specifies from whom the data are to be collected, when, and under what circumstances. How the study is designed affects the kinds of conclusions that can be drawn, (for example, whether we can claim that one thing is a cause of another).

Measurement is the process of determining values for each variable for each of the individuals in the sample. There are many different ways to gather data in social research and the data varies in quality. Three aspects of quality are discussed: discrimination, or the fineness of measurement; reliability, which determines the stability or replicability of the measurement; and validity, which is concerned with whether we are measuring what we want to measure and with whether the measurement is biased.

The chapter ends with a brief discussion of the steps necessary to the analysis of data.

These processes do not necessarily proceed in an orderly fashion in actual research. For example, in constructing the design or developing measurement procedures it may be found that the conceptualization of the problem is inadequate and needs to be carried further. Some movement back and forth among these processes usually takes place, although that is often not apparent in the published reports of research.

Notes

1. *Webster's Third New International Dictionary*, Springfield, Ma.: Merriam, 1965.
2. Richard A. Cloward and Lloyd E. Ohlin, *Delinquency and Opportunity*, Glencoe, Il.: Free Press, 1960.

Bibliography

Some introductory texts in research methods include:

Charles R. Atherton and David L. Klemmack, *Research Methods in Social Work: An Introduction*, Lexington, Ma.: Heath, 1982.

Earl R. Babbie, *The Practice of Social Research*, Belmont, Ca.: Wadsworth, 1975.

Kenneth D. Bailey, *Methods of Social Research*, 2nd ed. New York: Free Press, 1982.

Richard M. Grinnell, Ed., *Social Work Research and Evaluation*, Itasca, IL.: Peacock, 1981.

Fred N. Kerlinger, *Foundations of Behavioral Research*, New York: Holt, Rinehart and Winston, 1964.

Bernard S. Phillips, *Social Research: Strategy and Tactics*, 2d ed., New York: Macmillan, 1971.

Norman A. Polansky, *Social Work Research*, rev. ed., Chicago: University of Chicago Press, 1975.

William J. Reid and Audrey D. Smith, *Research in Social Work*, New York: Columbia University Press, 1981.

Claire Selltiz, Lawrence S. Wrightsman and Stuart W. Cook, *Research Methods in Social Relations*, 3d ed., New York: Holt, Rinehart and Winston, 1976.

H. W. Smith, *Strategies of Social Research*, Englewood Cliffs, NJ: Prentice-Hall, 1975.

Tony Tripodi and Irwin Epstein, *Research Techniques for Clinical Social Workers*, New York: Columbia University Press, 1980.

Tony Tripodi, Phillip Fellin and Henry J. Meyer, *The Assessment of Social Research*, Itasca, Il.: Peacock, 1969.

More technical books on research method include:

Thomas D. Cook and Donald T. Campbell, *Quasi-Experimentation*, Chicago: Rand McNally, 1979.

Abraham Kaplan, *The Conduct of Inquiry*, San Francisco: Chandler, 1964.

Comprehensive reviews of research include three volumes edited by Henry S. Maas published by the National Association of Social Workers, New York. The volumes are: *Five Fields of Social Service* (1966), *Research in the Social Services: A Five Year Review* (1971) and *Social Service Research: Reviews of Studies* (1978).

See also David Fanshel, Ed., *The Future of Social Work Research*, Washington, D. C.: National Association of Social Workers, 1980.

PART II

Using Research to Answer Practice Questions

3

Evaluation of Work with an Individual or Social System

In this chapter we discuss the evaluation of the core of human services practice: the determination of the impact of a worker's activities on individuals, families, groups, organizations, or communities. We hope to give readers some sense of how they can understand the effects of their own practice activities. We will develop many of these ideas in the context of working with individuals. However, most of these notions can be adapted for use in work with other social systems.

To begin, let us assume some problem has been identified and the practitioner is engaged in activities designed to help alleviate it. Most often some change is necessary, although we recognize that sometimes the practitioner is called upon to try to maintain things as they are, for example, when one tries to prevent the physical deterioration of an older person or the decline of a neighborhood. This chapter is about how one determines the effectiveness of one's actions and the factors influencing the outcome. This type of research is called *single case* or *single subject* research.

Specification

The most important idea in this chapter is specificity. We suggest that it is important to specify as clearly as possible three kinds of things: first, the problem and what it is one hopes to change; second, the intervention (what one is doing to bring about the change); and third, what other factors might bring about change or prevent it from happening.

SPECIFYING THE OBJECT OF CHANGE

The principal tasks in beginning work with an individual or family or with a larger social system such as an organization or community involve developing working relationships with the people concerned and determining the focus of the work to follow. Many textbooks on the methods of helping discuss these processes. We will not talk about them in detail, but we will discuss briefly the process of specifying the focus of work.

Work with an individual or other social system usually begins with a focus on a particular problem. Obviously, problems that face human service workers vary extensively in nature, scope, and origin. They may vary according to the number of people involved and the person who has identified the problem. Sometimes the problem is identified by the client (the primary individual with whom the worker is engaged) and sometimes by others. Sometimes the problem is very concrete, as when a client needs help in obtaining adequate housing. Other times, the problem may be rather abstract as when a young person expresses a need to find himself.

The initial statement of the problem is often vague, unclear, or amorphous, for example, a parent's complaint of difficulties in getting along with a child. The nature of the problem must be clarified before action can be taken, a process that takes place with the client through interactions in which the problem is explored and its various aspects identified. Often it is possible to break down problems into components or subproblems. It is desirable to understand something of the sources or causes of the situation at hand (although it is often not necessary to understand these in detail). Of course, there are often multiple problems present, and it may be necessary to focus on only one or two.

Once the problem is understood, the next step is to specify the objectives of the intervention. These should flow out of an understanding of the problem and be directed at eliminating it, reducing its impact, or adjusting those involved to the problem. That is, the objectives are to bring about some kind of change in the situation, for example, to reduce the frequency of a child's temper tantrums. Sometimes a deteriorating situation calls not for change but for attempts to stabilize matters. The objectives may be stated in terms of short- and long-range goals. It is therefore desirable to order objectives, and to specify which will be addressed first.

It is also desirable to specify objectives as concretely as possible, making them measurable or operational. At the end of intervention we want to be able to say whether or not our aims have been achieved. For example, we want to be able to say whether the frequency of tantrums has been reduced. We can be more confident that change has or has not occurred if the objectives can be measured in some way.

The indications of achieved objectives should (in principle, at least) be observable by more than one person. This is known as the principle of *consensual validation* of observations, if at least two people observe the same events and reach the same conclusions about them, we are more confident of the conclusions. Such agreement is possible only if indications of achievement of objectives are stated as clearly as possible. For example, we would want to define temper tantrum so that different people would agree on whether a tantrum has occurred.

We said above that it should be possible in principle for the indicators of change to be observable by another person. It is highly desirable that a person other than the primary worker in the case be available to provide consensual validation, but often that is not feasible and we are left with the observations of a single individual—usually the worker or sometimes the client. Such observations are, of course, suspect, since they may be affected by the worker's or client's investment in seeing change. But they are less suspect if they are based on relatively unambiguous indications of change which could be observed by another person.

Two problems are often raised in regard to the specification of objectives. First, objectives frequently change in the course of work with people. We might decide that the real problem is the relationship between the mother and father rather than the child's temper tantrums. When that happens, measures of the new objectives should be developed. However, if objectives seem to be changing constantly, almost from week to week, something may be wrong with the intervention. It is difficult to accomplish anything if one's aims are constantly shifting.

The second objection often raised to specification and measurement of objectives is that human problems are often difficult to pin down in measurable terms, presumably because problems are vague and complex. I believe that this difficulty is often overstated. Methods are available for measuring fairly complex human problems such as anxiety and depression. Beyond this, even when dealing with complicated problems, it is usually possible to identify one or more aspects of the problem that can be measured.

Usually the determination of change depends on a comparison of measurements of the extent of the problem before and after intervention. Measuring only after intervention usually is not sufficient to demonstrate that change has taken place unless the change is very dramatic, as for example, if the problem has completely disappeared. The measurement of the status of a problem before intervention is called the *baseline* measure. We will have more to say about baselines later on. One of the important principles in demonstrating change from such before-after measures is that the measurement procedures should be the same at both times. Otherwise, any differences observed might be due to changes in the measurements rather than in the problem situation. We would want to measure the number of temper tantrums before and after intervention in the same way at both times.

So the specification of objectives should lead to ways to measure change, usually in the problem situation. The description of a measurement of problem change includes three aspects: the nature of the problem, the source of the data on change, and the way in which the data are gathered.

Nature of the Problem. What is measured is, of course, determined by the nature of the problem. There are many problem classifications available with different emphases, ranging from psychiatric diagnoses to more socially oriented schemes. Here we will use a rather simple classification based on the location of the changes that are sought.

1. Resource needs. We include here changes in housing situation, finding a new job, obtaining public aid, acquiring a prosthesis, and so forth. Changes such as these are often quite easy to measure, since they are of the sort that a person desiring something either has or does not have it after intervention.
2. Changes in interactions between individuals. The most common of these problems concern family interactions such as those occurring between husband and wife or parent and child.
3. Changes in the individual. This includes changes in the individual's behavior (sometimes this overlaps with the previous category) and changes in attitudes or feelings (for example, depression, anxiety, or fears).

Sources of Data. Data on change can come from several sources. We will classify these in our work with individuals and families in terms of the individual from whom the information is obtained. Data may be obtained from the intervenor observing changes in behavior or emotions. Data may also be obtained from the client who might keep track of his own behavior or feelings. Finally, data may be obtained from other people in the client's environment.

When we are dealing with larger social systems like organizations or communities, the data may consist of information on economic trends or social indicators like delinquency rates or indices of family breakdown.

The Way in which Data is Gathered. Data are usually gathered in one of two ways:

1. Direct observation of behavior, that is, the observation by a researcher of the activities of an individual, family, or group.
2. Questionnaires administered in an interview or filled out by the client. Examples of questionnaires are problem inventories, symptom checklists and skills inventories. These methods of collecting data are discussed in detail in Chapter 10.

SPECIFICATION OF INTERVENTION PROCEDURES

Just as important as the specification of outcomes is the specification of the intervention. It does no good to discover that one
has been successful and not be able to describe reliably and in
detail what one has done.

After the objectives of intervention have been specified, the
proposed intervention procedures are described; that is, the plan
for proceeding is developed. Unfortunately, the actions actually
engaged in by the worker are rarely exactly as planned. Conditions change, the worker learns more about the situation, and the
intervention shifts to take account of these new developments.

The intervention as it is actually implemented, together with
all of its changes, should be documented as carefully as possible.
The criterion for a good specification of intervention is that it
should be possible for someone else to repeat the process on the
basis of the description provided. Sometimes we must depend on
the account of the worker to provide that description. At other
times it may be possible to monitor the intervention by external
means. For example, a worker or observer might make audio or
video tape recordings of interactions with a client. These can be
analyzed by raters to determine what actually occurred in the
sessions. It is certainly desirable to obtain external assessments of
what went on in intervention, although it is not always possible
to do so.

A number of instruments for rating the nature and quality of
intervention have been developed. For example, Rogers and his
colleagues have developed rating scales for what they consider to
be the core conditions of interpersonal treatment: the therapist's
empathy, warmth, and unconditional positive regard for the
client.[1]

SPECIFICATION OF OTHER FACTORS

The specification of other factors affecting change is more
problematic than specifying the hoped-for outcome or the intervention. Sometimes other factors are not explicitly recognized before the intervention is implemented, although it may be noted
that such and such will make it difficult to achieve the objectives
for the case. For example, economic stresses on the parents may

cause them to provoke the child's temper tantrums. It is important in the course of the intervention to note and keep a record of other things that are happening that might affect the outcome. This information becomes necessary if improvement occurs and it is possible that something besides the intervention caused the change. If improvement did not occur it will be useful to know what else happened, because those other things might have prevented the intervention from being successful.

Design

Our ultimate aim is to be able to say something about whether the intervention used was causally related to change in the problem situation. The first requirement is to show that change has occurred. As mentioned above, this usually requires that we have at least two measurements, one taken before and the other during or after the intervention. We might diagram this as shown in Figure 3.1. The diagram indicates that there has been a change for the better.

Unfortunately, data such as this do not necessarily mean that the intervention caused the change. There are lots of other explanations for this pattern of observations. Probably the simplest explanation is that the measures just happened to be taken at a time when the problem looked particularly bad (the baseline measure) or good (the post-intervention measure) and one or both observations are atypical of the period.

The usual way of dealing with these possibilities is to measure the problem at several times both before and after intervention. In that way we can be sure that the apparent change is not simply due to the time of measurement. We might diagram this as shown in Figure 3.2. The points in this diagram represent values of the measurement of the problem at various times—successive hours, days, weeks, or whatever. Notice that not all the points in each sector are at the same level. The measurement of a problem may fluctuate within each phase—people change from day to day for better or worse without the level of the underlying problem changing. Besides that, there is usually some error in the measurement, and the amount of error changes from one time to the next. A series of observations like this taken over time is called a *time series*.

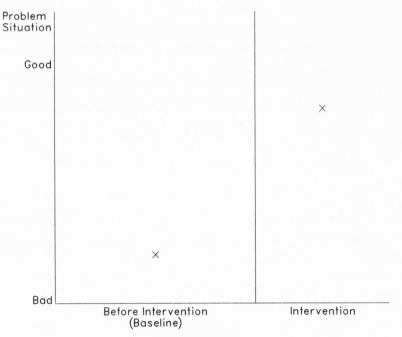

FIGURE 3.1

FIGURE 3.2

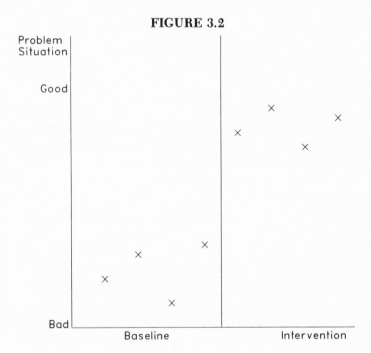

The diagrams above show a desired improvement (in behavior, feelings, and so forth) after intervention. Sometimes we want to decrease some undesired behavior or feeling. In that case we hope the diagram will look like that shown in Figure 3.3.

From a research point of view it is desirable that the baseline measures be stable, that is, that they not fluctuate too much or indicate impending improvement. If they fluctuate a lot, as in Figure 3.4, it will be difficult to tell if intervention has had an effect unless its impact is much greater than the fluctuations.

A sloping baseline would look like Figure 3.5. In this case, things seem to have been getting better even without intervention, so it is difficult to attribute the change to the intervention. From a clinical point of view the continued improvement is desirable, but it cannot be claimed that intervention was responsible for it.

The more measurements before and after intervention the better, from the standpoint of showing the effects of treatment. But in real treatment situations such an ideal often cannot be met. Indeed, it may not be possible to obtain even one baseline measurement, as when we are faced with a crisis situation in

FIGURE 3.3

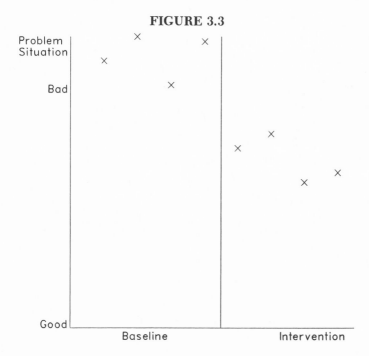

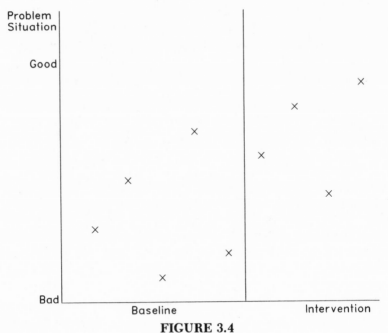

FIGURE 3.4

FIGURE 3.5

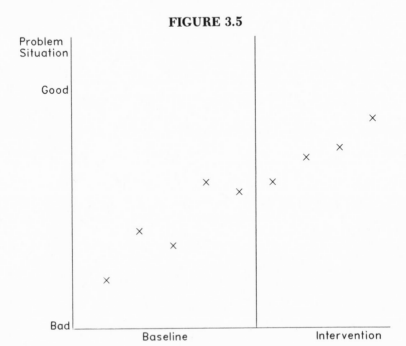

which something must be done immediately. Sometimes it is possible to reconstruct matters as they were before intervention (a retrospective baseline). Such baselines are somewhat suspect since they depend on the client's or somebody else's memory. Nonetheless, if this is the only option it's better than nothing.

Evaluation designs such as these, in which measurements are taken before and after intervention, are called *AB designs*. Such designs are not infallible in demonstrating the effects of treatment. Even with many observations before and after treatment and with a change in the problem we cannot be sure that the change occurred because of intervention. It is always possible that something else caused the change or that the individual was bound to get better anyway and just happened to do so at the time treatment was instituted. For example, our child with temper tantrums might mature, or perhaps a sibling might leave home at the time treatment is instituted.

This problem is particularly acute when we do not expect a change immediately at the point of intervention, but instead anticipate a delay before the effects of our actions appear. Then we get a pattern like that shown in Figure 3.6.

FIGURE 3.6

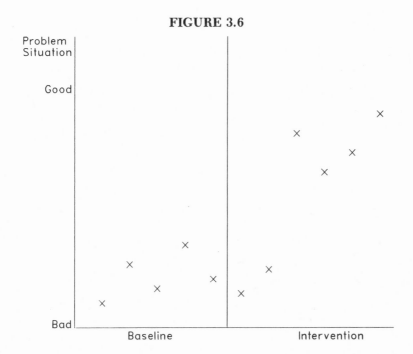

If a worker could specify beforehand how long it would take for the intervention to work, this pattern might be more convincing. Since that kind of prediction is hard to make, it is easy to argue that a change for the better was bound to occur sometime and it just happened to occur after the intervention started.

THE ABAB DESIGN

To counter this threat to causal conclusions, researchers have developed the so-called reversal, withdrawal, or ABAB design. In this design, baseline measurements are taken, the intervention is implemented for a period of time (until change occurs), then it is stopped for a time, and finally, it is reinstituted. Thus there are two periods of observations without intervention and two periods with intervention. The hoped-for results might be diagrammed as in Figure 3.7.

If the pattern is like this, the design is quite powerful in demonstrating that the intervention caused the change. It is quite unlikely that changes of this sort would have occurred because of other factors.

FIGURE 3.7

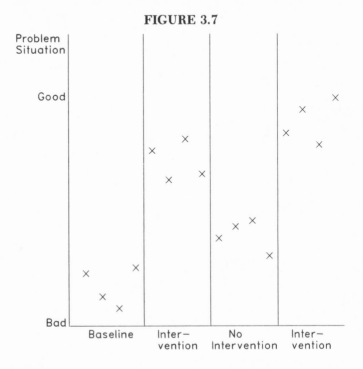

There are, however, a number of problems with the ABAB design. First of all, it depends on the problem getting better during the first treatment period, then getting worse during the second A period (when treatment is withdrawn), so that it can get better again during the ensuing period (the second B). Sometimes the problem does not become worse again during the second A period, so that no change has occurred in the last three periods. The diagram would then look like that shown in Figure 3.8. This result might mean one of two things. Either the treatment did not cause the change (instead, something else caused the effect) or the treatment did cause the change, but the change is enduring and cannot be reversed. It is impossible to tell which of these two explanations is the correct one.

A second problem with the ABAB design is that it is often not feasible or ethical to implement; the intervention may be such that it is not possible to stop it once it has begun or it would be unethical to do so. These factors limit the usefulness of the ABAB design in practice situations.

Extensions of AB and ABAB Designs. Researchers have developed a number of variations on the AB and ABAB designs,

FIGURE 3.8

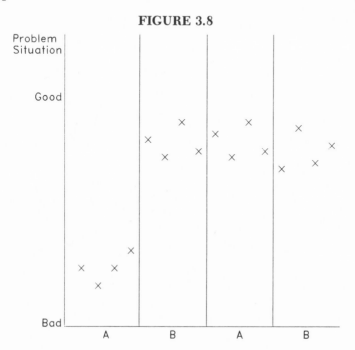

each intended to answer slightly different questions or for use under varying conditions. Many designs compare the effectiveness of two or more treatments. Most of these variations, however are not feasible in clinical situations, but they can be very useful in research settings in which the experimenter has greater control over conditions.[2]

MULTIPLE BASELINE DESIGNS

As we have seen, usually it is not possible to draw firm causal conclusions from the AB design, and the ABAB design often is not feasible. Another approach, the *multiple baseline design*, has been developed to enhance the plausibility of causal conclusions in clinical research. In this design, two or more problems are treated using the same approach, or the same problem is treated in two or more settings, or two or more persons with the same problem in the same setting are treated. The idea is to try the intervention out more than once, varying either the problem, the setting, or the individual. A baseline-intervention (AB) sequence is used in each situation. The design might be diagramed as in Figure 3.9.

FIGURE 3.9a   Situation 1

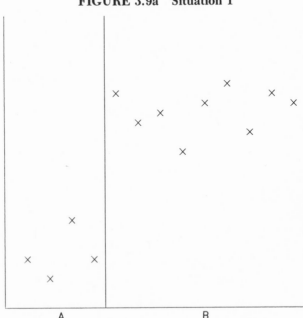

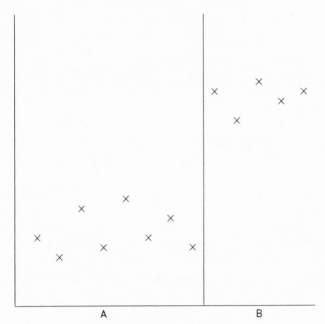

FIGURE 3.9b   Situation 2

FIGURE 3.9c   Situation 3

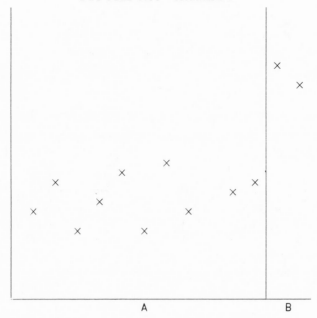

If improvement occurs each time following intervention, we have more confidence that the intervention caused the improvement than if we just tried it once.

In the multiple baseline design, only one of the three main factors (problem, setting, person) is different on each intervention occasion. The other two factors are held constant. A multiple baseline across problems might involve the successive treatment of a reading problem and a problem in learning arithmetic in the same child in the same classroom. A multiple baseline across settings might involve an attempt to reduce a child's hyperactivity first in a classroom then on a playground. A multiple baseline across persons might involve identical treatment in the same setting of a particular sexual dysfunction in two or more people. In all cases we would use the same treatment approach.

The idea behind the multiple baseline design is to try the intervention in more than one situation. Thus in multiple baselines across problems or settings it is important to stagger the timing of the intervention as shown in Figure 3.9. Otherwise, the interventions might be thought of as a single intervention and not as separate trials. In multiple baselines across people it is important to stagger the treatment if the individuals in question are in contact with each other and are likely to affect each other, as for example, if we are trying to treat two hyperactive friends in a classroom. In that case, the treatment of one may be the cause of any improvement in the other, rather than both of the individuals being independently affected by intervention. If the individuals have no contact with each other, it is not necessary to stagger treatments, although it may be desirable to make sure the treatment works with one person before trying it with another.

The issue we have just been discussing leads us to one of the major drawbacks in multiple baseline designs, the problem of generalization. It is entirely possible that treating a child's hyperactivity in the classroom will reduce it not only in the classroom but on the playground as well, without our ever paying attention to his behavior in the latter setting. When that happens, we say that *generalization* has taken place. Again, clinical and research interests conflict. The clinician will be properly happy if this happens, because the client has benefited doubly. But the design will have failed from a research point of view, because we did not get a chance to try the treatment twice.

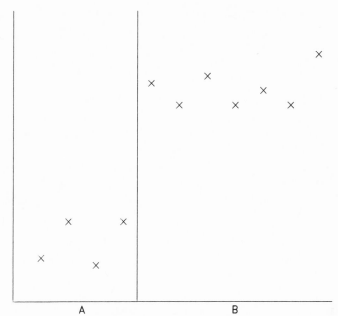

FIGURE 3.10a   Situation 1

FIGURE 3.10b   Situation 2

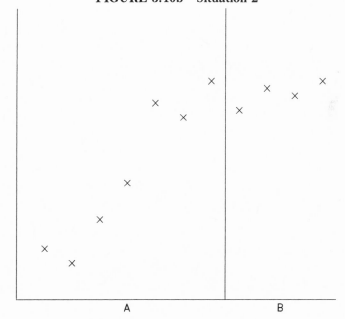

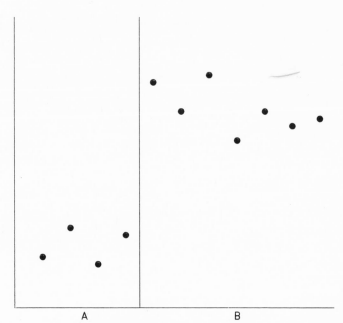

FIGURE 3.11a   Situation 1

FIGURE 3.11b   Situation 2

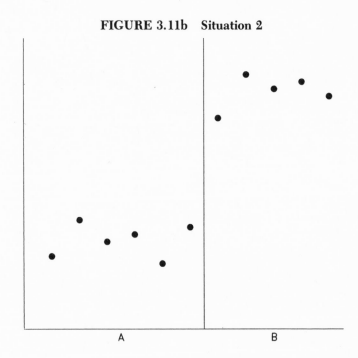

Although we will not try to interfere with beneficial generalization, we will try to gather data in such a way as to determine whether it has occurred. That is the reason that we begin baseline observations on all our situations at the same time (as indicated in Figure 3.9) even though we begin treatment at different times. If generalization has occurred we would expect the data to look like that shown in Figure 3.10. If we have independent effects the data should look like that found in Figure 3.11.

REPLICATION

Our discussion of multiple baseline designs brings us to the issue of the place of *replication* in research. In any research project involving one, several, or many individuals it is always possible for a critic to argue that the results are due to the particular people chosen for the study and would not be the same if other people were involved.

Science is concerned with generalizing, with finding out facts about the world that have some generality. The only way to be sure that a particular result lends itself to generalization is to try the treatment again. If it continues to work, each time we try it we have more confidence. Such a process is called replication. It is desirable to replicate studies of interventions no matter how many people are involved in the first study. This helps us to establish the effectiveness of an approach and to determine the limitations of the intervention.

In designing a replication, one of the major issues is that of how closely it should duplicate the original study. It cannot duplicate it exactly; at the very least, the time at which the replication is done will be different and probably the people and place of the study will be different also. It is desirable that such differences exist. In that way, if the replication comes up with the same results as the original study, we will be able to generalize, to assert that the intervention works in different situations.

But there is a problem here. If we vary the situation too much, we may not come out with the same results, because the treatment may not work in the new context. After all, no one treatment works for all problems, people, or situations. So a replication should be similar to the original study in some respects and different in others. Figuring out the necessary similarities and differences depends on one's knowledge of the field and on previous research. In general, a very new, untested approach ought to be tested first with replications that are very close to the original study. Subsequent replications should vary more and more of the conditions to seek greater generality.[3]

Replications in the social sciences are all too rare. There are several reasons for this. In the case of large scale studies involving a large sample, it is very expensive to repeat the research. Scientists are not inclined to repeat the discoveries of others; they would rather make discoveries of their own. Still another problem is that so-called negative results are rarely published. If an intervention doesn't work in a particular situation, few people will hear about it, despite the fact that it is important to know the limits of techniques.

In the physical sciences experimental results are replicated more often than in the social sciences. Whenever someone publishes an important new finding in the physical sciences, someone else runs to his laboratory to try it out. Part of the reason for this difference is economics. In the physical sciences there is usually more than one laboratory capable of performing a particular experiment. Most of the costs of a discovery are in the equipment and in the processes leading up to the actual experiment, that is, the time of the experimenter and his assistants in thinking through the problem and in lots of trials that don't work out. Once an experimenter has his discovery, he reveals in print how he got it, and others can repeat it if they have the equipment. The costs of obtaining the data for a replication are relatively low. In the social sciences the reverse is true. Thus although a replication costs less than an original study (because the original conceptualization and the measurement techniques have already been worked out), it is still very expensive.

Assessment of Data

The assessment of data from single subject designs proceeds in two stages. It is necessary to determine first if a change has occurred, and then, if any changes observed are likely to be due to intervention.

The first step in the first stage is to plot the data in diagrams similar to those presented earlier in this chapter. Often, this is as far as formal data analysis goes. The diagram is inspected to determine whether a shift in level or a shift in slope has occurred. The major problem with this procedure is that what appear to be changes may just be random fluctuations in behavior. The fewer the observations in each stage and the greater the variation in the observations, the more difficult it is to argue that a change has taken place. For example, suppose we are dealing with a child who is given to frequent temper tantrums. We might have a diagram like that shown in Figure 3.12. Although the number of tantrums is less on the days within the treatment phase, it would be difficult to argue that a real change has taken place, because more observations may not continue to show fewer tantrums. The number of tantrums per day was varying somewhat before treatment, and it is possible that the two observations taken after treatment began were on days that just happened to have fewer tantrums.

FIGURE 3.12

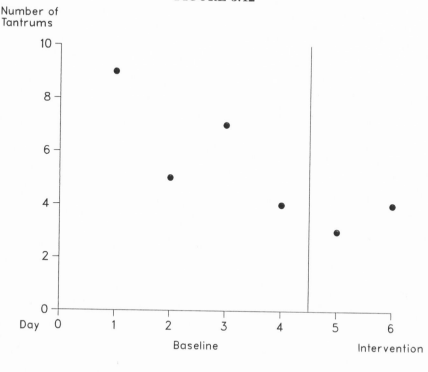

Therefore, a conclusion that a change has taken place is more convincing the more observations we have in each phase. It is also more convincing if the behavior is relatively constant within phases. We would be more assured of a change by diagram A than by diagram B in Figure 3.13.

So far we have considered only changes in level of behavior. It is also possible that the slopes of the rates of behavior might change. That is, during baseline or treatment gradual improvement or deterioration might take place.

When the behavior deteriorates during baseline and then starts improving during treatment the diagram looks like that shown in Figure 3.14. It seems clear that in this situation a change has occurred. If the opposite happens—improvement during baseline and deterioration during treatment—we can also be clear that a change has occurred, although we cannot be happy about the outcome.

Other situations involving changes in slope are more problematic to interpret. Some examples are:

1. Improvement during baseline with an increased rate of improvement during treatment, as shown in Figure 3.15. In this case it usually is difficult to be sure things really have changed with treatment. It is possible that the trend of the behavior without treatment would have looked like that shown in Figure 3.16.
2. Deterioration during baseline with lessened deterioration during treatment is illustrated in Figure 3.17. This is essentially the reverse of the previous situation.
3. We can also have combinations of slopes and flat lines. Sometimes these are interpretable as real changes and other times not. For example, we might have deterioration in baseline and then, during treatment, stabilization at a somewhat higher level than the last baseline point, as in Figure 3.18. In this case, change does seem to have occurred.

Another example is improvement during baseline with a jump during treatment to a stable level, as in Figure 3.19. Here it is difficult to assert that real change occurred during treatment, since the behavior seemed to be improving with or without treatment.

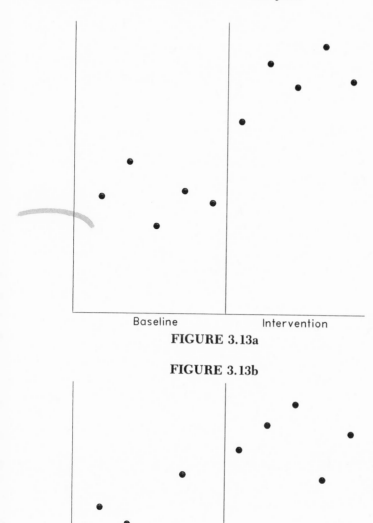

Baseline   Intervention

FIGURE 3.13a

FIGURE 3.13b

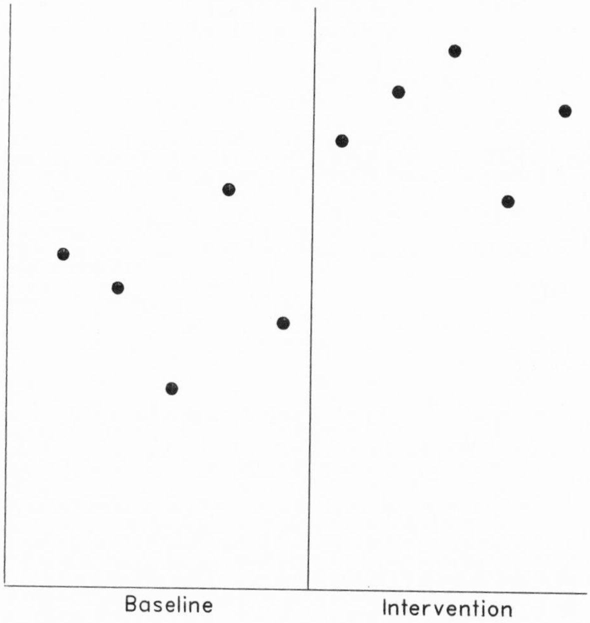

Baseline   Intervention

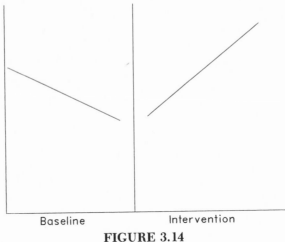

FIGURE 3.14

Multiple phase designs like the ABAB and multiple baseline require that several judgments on change be made, one for each shift in phase (that is, for each change from baseline to treatment and vice versa).

The determination of whether change has taken place is a matter of judgment, judgment that can be questioned in many cases. Statisticians have attempted to develop techniques for analysis of data from such studies that would remove the judgmental aspects

FIGURE 3.15

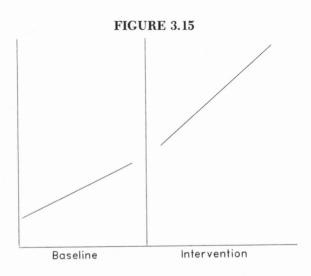

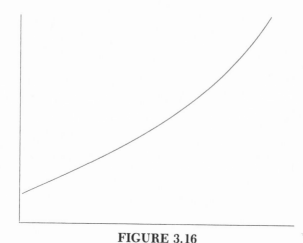

FIGURE 3.16

by subjecting the data to mechanical procedures. Unfortunately, all such techniques have limitations. Some require that we make assumptions about the data that often are not reasonable. Others are quite complicated mathematically and in addition require that we have many observations in each phase. In my view, it is unlikely that many practitioners will make much use of these techniques and will depend instead on visual inspection of diagrams, recognizing its limitations.

If our judgment is that change has occurred, it is necessary to

FIGURE 3.17

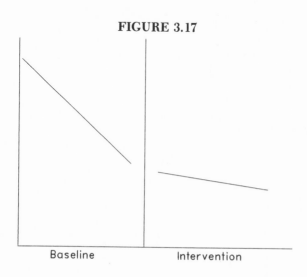

Baseline   Intervention

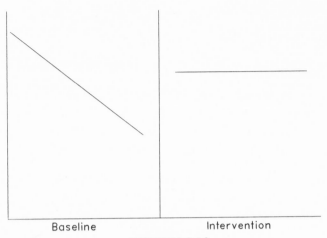

Baseline   Intervention

FIGURE 3.18

move on to the second stage in analysis, deciding whether the change can be attributed to the intervention. Even if change occurred, it is possible that it was due to factors other than the intervention.

Theoretically, if one has used an ABAB design or one of its variations and the data show clear and consistent differences between the A and the B conditions, one can be fairly certain that intervention caused the changes. As indicated earlier, such designs are the most effective for proving causal connections.

FIGURE 3.19

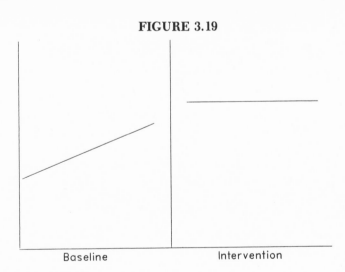

Baseline   Intervention

Multiple baseline designs are the next most convincing. Here the threats to causal conclusions depend on whether the design is across individuals, settings, or behaviors. If the design is across individuals, it is always possible that we chose individuals that responded to some factor other than treatment at about the same time treatment was initiated. For settings or behaviors it is possible that the changes are due to generalization even though treatment effects coincided with each introduction of treatment. These possibilities must be considered as alternatives to the explanation that change occurred because of treatment. In a particular situation it may be unlikely that these alternative explanations are correct. Other times it may be impossible to chose which of the explanations is most likely, and we may be unable to assert that treatment was effective.

Unfortunately, the most common design, the AB, is the least convincing in demonstrating treatment effectiveness. Even if change has occurred subsequent to instituting treatment, one can almost always think of several explanations for this change other than treatment. Our approach to this problem is to try to think of all the possible or at least plausible alternative explanations and to try to reason from knowledge of the situation how likely each is. Again, we will often be left with one or more possible explanations other than treatment. Our only hope then is to replicate the treatment with another client to see if change occurs again.

Example of a Single Subject Research Study

An example of the procedures discussed in this chapter is contained in an article titled "Cognitive-Behavior Modification Treatment of an Aggressive 11 year-old Boy."[4] The study involved work with a single child in a small residential treatment center. The specification of the problem was uncontrolled hitting, fighting and swearing in response to slight provocations. Previous efforts to change the behavior had been unsuccessful.

The intervention rested on the theory that the provocative stimulus was followed immediately by the aggressive behavior. The intervention was aimed at getting the child to control his behavior by having him pause between provocation and action to think about the reasons for his anger and the consequences of aggressive responses. This was done through the procedures of verbal self-instruction and self-monitoring. In *verbal self-instruction* the client explained to himself either out loud or covertly why he was angry, that he should not respond aggressively, and how he might respond more appropriately. The client also rewarded himself by self-praise when he was successful. In *self-monitoring* the client kept track (in a small notebook) of the incidents in which he was angry.

The aggressive behaviors of hitting, fighting, and swearing were carefully defined and recorded by child care workers in the institution. Reliability was checked by the treatment worker on two occasions during the study. That is, the worker was present on those occasions to rate aggressive behavior of the child. The author reports that both times there was 100 percent agreement between observers (exactly how this percentage agreement was calculated was not reported).

A multiple baseline design over behaviors (hitting, fighting, and swearing) was planned. The design included a two-week baseline period before treatment began in which data was collected on the incidence of behaviors. Treatment was continued for four weeks. The first behavior addressed in treatment was fighting. When treatment began, the incidence of fighting dropped substantially. Unfortunately for the research, but fortunately for the child, generalization occurred and the incidence of hitting and swearing also dropped at the same time. A statistical analysis helped confirm that there had been a change in behavior.

This study is a good example of the use of single case designs in therapeutic situations. It also illustrates the limitations of the procedures. The fact that behavior change took place seems to be well established, but it is not possible to show conclusively that the intervention was the cause of that change, because of the failure of the multiple baseline design. It is possible that the boy might have changed anyway, because he was maturing or because something else happened besides the intervention. Demonstration of the efficacy of these particular procedures will depend on replications. Such replications, together with the results of this study, will indicate whether these techniques have general applicability.

Summary

This chapter has focused on how a professional can evaluate his work with individuals or social systems. Such studies often make use of single subject or single case designs. First we must specify the problem and the goals for intervention. Such specification should result in objectives that are measurable so that we can verify whether change has taken place.

Next the intervention processes must be specified. The intervention must be monitored and fully described to compare plans with actual execution.

The confidence we have in attributing change in the problem to a specific intervention depends on the design of the study. Three common designs have been discussed in this chapter; the AB, ABAB, and multiple baseline. ABAB designs are most convincing in asserting causal connections but are difficult to implement and thus are used less often. AB designs are least convincing but are the most common because of the relative ease of carrying them out.

This chapter has also considered the problems of generalization and the role of replication in building our confidence in the generality of research findings. Finally, problems in the interpretation of data from single subject studies have been discussed.

Notes

1. Carl R. Rogers, Eugene T. Gendlin, Donald J. Kiesler, and Charles B. Truax, *The Therapeutic Relationship and its Impact*, Madison, Wi.: University of Wisconsin Press, 1967.

2. Michel Hersen and David H. Barlow, *Single Case Experimental Designs*, New York: Pergamon Press, 1976.

3. Murray Sidman, *Tactics of Scientific Research: Evaluating Experimental Data in Psychology*, New York: Basic Books, 1960.

4. Sara Mansfield Taber, Cognitive-Behavior Modification Treatment of an Aggressive 11-year-old Boy, *Social Work Research and Abstracts*, 17(2):13-23, 1981.

Bibliography

Some books and articles that discuss single subject research methods
are:

Gene V. Glass, Vernon L. Willson, and John N. Gottman, *Design and
Analysis of Time Series Experiments*, Boulder, Co.: Colorado Associated University Press, 1975.

John M. Gottman and Sandra R. Leiblum, *How to do Psychotherapy
and How to Evaluate it*, New York: Holt, Rinehart and Winston,
1974.

Michel Hersen and David H. Barlow, *Single Case Experimental Designs*, New York: Pergamon Press, 1976.

Michael W. Howe, Casework Self-Evaluation: A Single Subject Approach, *Social Service Review*, 48:10-15, 1974.

Srinika Jayaratne and Rona L. Levy, *Empirical Clinical Practice*, New
York: Columbia University Press, 1979.

Thomas R. Kratochwill, Ed., *Single Subject Research*, Academic Press,
New York, 1978.

Elsie M. Pinkston, John L. Levitt, Glenn R. Green, Nick L. Linsk, and
Tina Rzepnicki, *Effective Social Work Practice: A Scientific Approach to Helping*, San Francisco: Jossey-Bass Publishers, 1982.

Murray Sidman, *Tactics of Scientific Research*, New York: Basic Books,
1960.

Edwin J. Thomas, Research and Service in Single-Case Experimentation: Conflicts and Choices, *Social Work Research and Abstracts*,
14(4):20-31,1978.

John S. Wodarski, *The Role of Research in Clinical Practice*, Baltimore:
University Park Press, 1981.

Another study using a single subject design is:

Neal Broxmeyer, Practitioner Research in Treating a Borderline Child,
Social Work Research and Abstracts, 14(4):5-11, 1978.

4

Group Designs and the Evaluation of Programs

In this chapter we turn from research which focuses on one or a few individuals to research in which a number of individuals, families, or other social entities are studied at the same time. We place our discussion in the context of evaluation of programs, although these procedures are used to answer other types of questions requiring the study of numbers of people. The kind of research discussed here is often called _group research_.

Why should we study groups of people all at once rather than one at a time? The principal reason is that people are different, and thus we are never able to say anything about all people from having studied one person. As has been said before, an individual is like all people in some ways, like some people in other ways, and unlike all other people in still other ways. In a study of a single individual, we are not able to say definitively which characteristics are unique and which are common to others. The problem is often summed up by saying that we cannot generalize from the study of a single case.

So we use group studies to attempt to generalize, to be able to talk about things that are common for groups of people. We

63

also use group studies to determine how much variation there is among people.

There are advantages and limitations to both single case and group studies. Although we are able to generalize with the latter, we loose the ability to study individuals in detail. This problem can be overcome in single case studies. Hence both individual and group studies must be used to advance knowledge about effective practice.

Group studies are particularly appropriate when we want to assess the effectiveness of whole programs. By a whole program we mean a set of interventions, techniques, or procedures (an intervention package) that is used with a group of people. Usually the people in the group are experiencing the same or similar problems. All the interventions are available to everyone in the group, although not all will be used by everyone.

For example, suppose that a family service agency has established a program designed to prevent the institutionalization of older people in a particular community. After analysis of the reasons for institutionalization, the agency designs a program that has a number of components: medical assistance, home delivered meals, recreational opportunities, and counseling for the older person and his or her family. The agency wants to evaluate the program, to test its effectiveness. We will follow the steps in designing and implementing such an evaluation.

Measurement

Although the agency might not begin planning the evaluation by thinking about measurement problems, measurement is so important in evaluation and other kinds of social research that we begin with it here.

First, we consider measurement of the *outcome* variable (also called the dependent or criteria variable). The objective of the program is to prevent institutionalization, so we must specify what we mean by institutionalization. It may not seem to be very complicated; we need only to determine whether a client has gone into an institution. But matters are not quite that simple. Institutionalization is an event that may happen now or later. Probably we will not be willing to observe each individual from now until death to see if he or she is institutionalized. So we need to decide on the period of time we will wait to see if institutionalization occurs. There are lots of possibilities. We could observe for the time the person is active in the program, for two years after leaving the program, until the person is eighty years old, and so forth.

Further, we ought to make clear what we mean by institutionalization. Do we mean a nursing home or hospital? What about sheltered care facilities, group living arrangements with little supervision, or apartment houses for the elderly? Do we include hospitalization for acute medical conditions like broken bones, or do we mean only institutionalization that is expected to last for a long time? The answers to these questions require careful thought with reference to the objectives and the content of the program.

Beyond that, it is likely that the agency will be interested in more than whether institutionalization occurs within some period of time. It may consider its work at least partially successful if institutionalization occurred but was delayed. Thus another measure of outcome might be the number of months the individual was in the community during a particular period of time.

But it is unlikely that anyone would be satisfied with an evaluation of a program that depended only on institutionalization as an outcome measure. More likely, other aspects of the individual's life would be examined—perhaps social functioning, life satisfaction, psychological health, or any one of a number of other variables. It is generally desirable to have a number of measures of outcome. No one measure can tell us everything, because all have at least some flaws. However, an evaluator cannot look at all possible outcome measures, so selections must be made on the basis of those that most fit with the objectives and content of the program.

The researcher may need to develop measures for a particular evaluation project or he or she may be able to use one of a number of instruments that have already been developed. Measuring instruments exist for variables like social functioning, psychological health, life satisfaction, and many others.

MEASUREMENT OF THE INDEPENDENT VARIABLE

As with the dependent variable, it may seem initially that there is no problem in measuring the independent variable; an individual either receives the service or not. Again, matters are often not that clear-cut. Persons may receive more or less of the service (a few or many interviews, for example), and in a multi-faceted program such as our example, may receive some elements of the program and not others. So it is important to document what services each individual received and how much: how many times did he or she attend recreational activities, how many counseling sessions were held, and what was the content of the counseling?

It is important to find out to what extent the program was implemented as planned. Few programs are conducted in the way they were originally planned: the exigencies of environmental constraints, budget limitations, and simply the ability and imagination of those responsible will always result in variations from the original conception.

Many program evaluations are disappointing because they fail to demonstrate the effectiveness of the program. However, often the program studied is not the program as it was originally planned. Part of the responsibility of the program evaluator, whether the results are good, bad, or in between, is to describe fully the program that was evaluated as it was implemented, not as it was designed. As in the last chapter, the criteria for this is whether someone else could develop a similar program on the basis of the description.

Design

The second critical aspect of a group evaluation is the structure of the research. Assuming that the measurements are adequate, the design determines the kinds of conclusions that can be reached. In an evaluation context, the design determines the extent to which we can conclude that any changes in the problem were due to the intervention.

The Single Group Design

The simplest kind of design is the single group design. In terms of our example, a group of individuals would be invited to participate in the program. The outcome for each individual (for example, whether they were institutionalized and how long they stayed in the community) would be measured. If the status of each individual on one or more variables (for example, social functioning) is measured before and after the intervention, the design is called a before-after single group design.

Single group designs are extremely limited in the conclusions that may be drawn from them. Suppose that 30 percent of our clients were institutionalized within a year after starting the program. Do we call that a success or a failure? We can't call it a failure, because no matter how good the program is, it is likely that a few older people will have to be institutionalized. How many is a few? Is 30 percent too many? Nor can we call it a success just because 70 percent stayed out of institutions. How can we know they wouldn't have stayed out even without our program?

Single group designs suffer from the lack of comparisons. Without something with which to compare the results, we have problems in drawing conclusions. Therefore, it is better to have a design in which we compare persons who received the service with those who did not. It is best to build such a comparison into the design of the study from the beginning. We will discuss such designs below, but before doing so, we will consider ways to make use of the single group design.

Sometimes comparisons can be made with data outside this program. If it is known from other studies or from census data what proportion of older people are institutionalized, that information could be compared with the experience of our study participants.

While such comparisons may be instructive, it is quite dangerous to depend on them too much. The problem is that the group of old people involved in our project may not be similar to our comparison group. They may not be representative of old people as a whole, or they may not have the same characteristics as those in the other studies. For example, our group as a whole may be healthier or may have stronger family ties. Thus if the project group had lower institutionalization rates than the comparison, it is possible that such lower rates were due to these factors rather than the program. Similarly, if the project group had higher rates, it is possible that the group was not as well off to begin with and might have done even worse without the service.

Another way to deal with single group designs is to try to make use of differences within the group in the amount of service received. In most social programs people get varying amounts of service. Thus it would be possible to compare the outcomes of those who received lots of service with those who received little.

Again, there are severe difficulties in such comparisons. Suppose those who got more service did better than those who did not. There are almost always several explanations for this difference other than amount of service. Possibly those who got more service were healthier or better motivated or had more family supports and thus would have gotten better anyway. Sometimes researchers try to control for such alternative explanations through statistical analysis of the data, but this is rarely fully convincing.

Still another approach to single group designs is to follow each case closely throughout the period of the program (this is almost like treating each case as a single case in a time series design). We identify exactly when each intervention is given and when changes occur in the individual. The hope is that causal relationships may be understood by studying the order of events over time. While this approach may be useful in certain circumstances, it has a number of difficulties. The effects of social interventions are often delayed, and it is hard to assert that an intervention caused a change sometime later. All the problems outlined in the previous chapter in connection with the AB design apply here.

Multiple Group Designs

As indicated above, it is desirable to incorporate one or more comparison groups into the design. There are basically two ways to do this; the first involves a naturally occurring comparison group and the second, a randomized experimental design.

NATURALLY OCCURRING COMPARISON GROUPS

Again using our example, we might accept a number of persons into our program and then go out into the community to find a group of elderly people not involved in the program. We would then apply our outcome measures to both groups and compare the results.

The validity of this approach rests on the similarity of the two groups at the outset. It is often very difficult to find a group of persons who are comparable to the group being treated and to prove that they are or are not comparable. In our example we want to have two groups that are equally in need of the services (although only one group will receive them). Beyond that, we would want them to be equally likely to be institutionalized within the period of our study—a comparison which would be extremely difficult to support.

Sometimes elaborate efforts are undertaken to try to make the two groups comparable, either as whole groups or as matched pairs of persons from each group. In our example we might try to make our two groups of older people comparable with regard to physical condition, a task which often proves difficult. Achieving that, however, we cannot be sure that the groups will not be different on other unidentified variables that are important for the outcome. Again, statistical analysis can compensate for these problems, but only partially.

RANDOMIZED EXPERIMENTAL DESIGNS

The only way to assure that the groups are as comparable as possible is through the use of a randomized experimental design. In this design a group of individuals who want and need the services of the program are identified and divided into two groups, one receiving service and the other not receiving it. The assignment to these two groups takes place randomly; that is, some mechanical process (like the flip of a coin) governs the placement of persons in the groups and human judgment is not allowed to interfere. The group receiving the experimental service is called the *experimental* group, the other is called the *control* group. Usually they are made equal in size, although this is not essential.

Such a process assures that the differences between the groups will be random. Thus the possibility is reduced that differences in the groups at the outset will explain differences after the intervention. The larger the groups and the more homogeneous the population from which we select them the better the random process works in assuring their equality. Even with random assignment, it is possible that differences at the conclusion of treatment may not be due to treatment, but statistical analysis can tell us how likely that is.

Although the randomized experimental design is theoretically the best way to be sure that we can reach conclusions about the effectiveness of programs, it is not without its problems. Some of these are:

1. *Differential loss of subjects*. In most research studies that take place over a period of time, some subjects drop out. Often more persons will drop out of one group. Even if about the same number of persons drop out of each group, the process does not occur randomly (human decisions are involved) so the groups can no longer be claimed to be similar (the differences between the groups at the end of intervention might be due to differences in the persons who dropped out). Sometimes the dropout problem is negligible and can be ignored, other times ways can be found to adjust for it through statistical analysis. Frequently, however, it threatens the development of solid conclusions from the study.

2. *Differential reactivity to measures*. It is usually desirable to have measurements of things like social functioning both before and after the service so that the amount of change can be determined. When we do this, however, we run the risk that the process of measuring individuals before service may have some impact on them. Measurement may sensitize persons to the service, and thus differences in outcome may be the result of a combination of the measurement and the service rather than the service alone. This is called an interaction of measurement and treatment. Sometimes this problem is handled by having an additional comparison group. The additional comparison group is measured only at the end and thus cannot be affected by a pretreatment measurement.

3. *Ethical problems*. The experimental design as described above requires that a group of clients be denied service, at least for a while. The implications of this are discussed more fully in Chapter 8; briefly, the conflict concerns the ethical questionability of withholding treatment in an experimental situation. Sometimes the ethical problem is dealt with by providing the control group with some service, perhaps a well-established service. Of course, in this situation the experimental service is

not being compared with no service but rather with some other service, in the hope that it will be superior. This approach sometimes makes it more difficult to detect an experimental effect (since two treatments rather than treatment and nontreatment are being compared), but the ethical problems may be less.

4. *Experimental leakage.* Sometimes in studies of services the control group turns out not to have been an untreated group. That is, the control group may receive some service, somehow. Persons denied service by the research agency may go someplace else. If this happens, the difference in outcome between our experimental group and the control group may be less than if the control group did not receive any service.

At times researchers try to reduce the effects of the last problem by providing an alternative service, perhaps a placebo service. A *placebo service* is one in which clients believe they are getting help, but the service is theoretically ineffective. In some circumstances placebo service may be given for a short while before starting the real service.

Placebo groups are also used to try to separate specific from nonspecific effects of the service. For example, one of the components of our program is counseling on personal problems. The architects of our program might have thought that counseling would be helpful in giving persons needed advice and information. However, in the process of providing this, the counselor is paying attention to the individual. The attention, concern, and interest displayed may be the effective elements of the counseling, rather than the advice and information. Hence a control group receiving attention but not advice and information might be introduced into the design to sort things out.

VARIATIONS ON EXPERIMENTAL DESIGNS

There are many variations on the randomized experimental-control group design, some of which have been mentioned above.

Before-after Measurement. Theoretically, the process of random assignment produces nearly equivalent groups before treatment (or to be more precise, groups that differ only randomly). If that is the case, it should be necessary to measure both groups only at the end of service, or at some appropriate follow-up point. If there are substantial differences between the groups at that point, the differences should be due to the experimental intervention.

However, particularly with small samples, it is possible for the groups to be somewhat different before intervention, even with random assignment. Thus it is desirable to have measures of the outcome variables before treatment begins in order to determine whether such differences are present. In our example, if we randomly assigned twenty old people to the experimental intervention and twenty to an untreated control group, it is possible that those in the experimental group might have been healthier than those in the control group. If there are such differences, it is not legitimate to switch cases from one group to another (thus replacing random selection with our own judgment). Instead, emphasis should be placed on comparing amounts of change rather than status at the end of service.

Before-after designs also allow us to understand more fully the results of the study. In our study, having measures of, for example physical health at the beginning of service would allow us to say something about the effects of health on outcome; we could compare healthier persons in the experimental group with similar persons in the control group and then do the same with persons not so healthy to see how the service works differently depending on physical condition.

Whenever we use comparison groups that are not randomly assigned we should try to have before measures. Since the groups probably do differ before treatment our analysis will depend on change rather than on a comparison of levels of functioning after the treatment.

Designs with More Than Two Groups. We have already mentioned multiple group designs as a way of handling the problem of before measurement effects. That is, if we think that the before measurement has some effect on people, we might have one control group with before measurement and another without. More than two groups are often used for other purposes as well. For example, we might want to compare one intervention with another and at the same time compare both with an untreated control group.

A more complex version of this is a *multifactorial* design in

which various combinations of interventions are systematically investigated. For example, we might be interested in the effects of
recreational service and counseling together and separately. We
would need four groups to undertake the study, as shown in Table 4.1.

TABLE 4.1

	No Recreation	*Recreation*
No counseling	Neither recreation nor counseling	Recreation only
Counseling	Counseling only	Counseling and recreation

One of the advantages of this design is that it allows for the
application of a powerful set of statistical procedures known as
the *analysis of variance*.

Matched Pairs Designs. Sometimes researchers develop a
set of matched pairs of individuals, then randomly assign one
member of each pair to the experimental treatment and the other
to the control condition. The individuals are matched on characteristics that are thought to be related to outcome, for example,
motivation or seriousness of problem. This procedure usually im-
proves the possibility of finding an effect of the intervention. The
analysis of the data is done on differences between pairs, rather
than differences in averages between whole groups. This is quite
different from constructing matched pairs after one of the cases is
already in the experimental group, a procedure mentioned earlier. Matching before assignment to treatment (with the assignment being done randomly) can be very effective, while matching
after the fact is usually much less useful from the standpoint of
being able to draw causal conclusions.

Despite their advantages, matched pair designs are often hard
to implement. The variables on which the matching takes place
must be related to the outcome for the procedure to be effective.
(Sometimes cases are matched on variables like sex and age, but
if these are not related to outcome the matching will be useless.)
It is often difficult to find matches, and persons who do not match
someone else must be eliminated from the study. Thus the group
of matched pairs that remains is often not representative of the
population from which it was drawn.

Data Analysis

Let us suppose in the example we have used in this chapter that we had a group of forty clients who received our service and we observed a group of sixty older people who did not receive our service. For the moment it does not matter whether we had a formal experimental design with random assignment or merely a nonrandom comparison group. To simplify things, suppose that we have two outcome measures on all 100 persons: first, whether they were institutionalized within two years and second, the number of months they were institutionalized during the two year period.

We now ask whether the group receiving service did better than the group that did not receive service. We will answer this question by looking at the differences in the two groups on our two measures. No matter how good our service was, we do not expect that everybody who received service was able to stay out of institutions, so we will compare the two groups as to how many were institutionalized and for how long. We will start with lists of the members of the two groups showing whether they were institutionalized and if institutionalized, the number of months each person spent in institutions. But it is difficult to tell anything from such lists, so we need some way to summarize the information so that we can compare the two groups more readily. The way we make those summaries is different for the two variables.

The first variable, whether institutionalized, is called a _categorical_ (or _nominal_) variable because it has subgroups. The analysis of such variables usually begins with a table, sometimes called a crosstabulation, crosstab, or crossbreak. This may look like Table 4.2.

TABLE 4.2

	Institutionalized	Not Institutionalized	Total
In program	12	28	40
Not in program	25	35	60
Total	37	63	100

The numbers in the cells are numbers of people; for example, twelve people who were in the program were institutionalized.

As is stands, it is hard to make comparisons between the program group and the nonprogram group from this table. It is not useful to compare directly the number of persons institutionalized in the program group (twelve) with those institutionalized in the nonprogram group (twenty-five). The two groups are of different sizes, the twelve institutionalized were taken from a group of forty and the twenty-five from a group of sixty. To get around this problem we use percentages; we find what percent (ten) is of forty and what percent twenty-five is of sixty. We can then construct a table (Table 4.3) with this information.

TABLE 4.3

	Institutionalized	Not Institutionalized	Total
In program	30%	70%	40
Not in program	42%	58%	60

Now we can compare the 30 percent with the 42 percent and conclude that in our sample those people in the program were less often institutionalized than those not in the program. On this measure the people in the program did better than those who were not in the program.

For the second measure, the number of months institutionalized, one approach would be to develop categories for this variable and then construct another table which might look like Table 4.4.

TABLE 4.4   Length of Institutionalization in Months

	None	Less than	2 to 6	More Than	Total
In program	28	6	4	2	40
Not in program	35	8	10	7	60
Total	63	14	14	9	100

We could then compute percentages and again make comparisons, although the latter will be more difficult, since there are more figures involved.

Another way to look at variables like number of months is in terms of averages (called *means* by statisticians). We can find averages for the number of months individuals in each group were institutionalized and compare those averages. Suppose for our data the averages were: in program, 1.05 months and not in program, 1.97 months. Again we find that the program group did better, since they had a smaller average length of institutionalization.

INFERENCE

So far our analysis has been confined to what is called descriptive statistics or descriptive data analysis. This allows us to say whether the groups we studied were different, whether they were different in the way we expected (that is, whether program or nonprogram people did better), and how much of a difference there was (for example, the difference in those institutionalized was 12 percent). Sometimes that is enough, but we may want to go further. Often we want to be able to draw conclusions about a larger group of people than those we happened to study, generalizing beyond the present sample. We want to be able to say that it is likely similar results would be found if we were to repeat the study or if we were to establish our program on a broader basis.

To proceed with drawing such conclusions, it is necessary to think of the groups we studied as samples from larger groups called *populations* or *universes*. Sometimes the populations are hypothetical. In our case the group that received service must be thought of as a sample from a hypothetical population of persons who have received service or might receive service in the future. Usually it is necessary to think of the groups we studied as random samples from their populations. Unfortunately, even if it is random, a sample is never completely representative of the population from which it is drawn. However, we attempt to draw conclusions (or make inferences) on the basis of this data. The branch of statistics concerned with drawing conclusions about a population on the basis of a sample is called *inferential statistics*.

Inferential statistics has two principal branches called hypothesis testing and confidence interval construction. The two are closely related. *Hypothesis testing* is concerned with determining whether certain statements about the population (hypotheses) are likely to be true or false. For example, we might have the following hypothesis: Persons in a program like this are less often institutionalized than persons not in a program. *Confidence interval construction* involves finding two numbers within which we expect a population characteristic to lie. For example, we might say that it is likely that the difference between the means of lengths of hospitalization for program and nonprogram groups lies between *a* and *b*.

In both hypothesis testing and confidence interval construction we wind up with conclusions that are not certain or absolutely true, but rather are probabilistic. For example, we might say that the probability that there is a difference in proportions institutionalized is .95 (or 95 percent) or that there is a .95 probability that the population mean lies between *a* and *b*. (Technically we must say that the population mean will lie in the interval computed 95 percent of the times we use this procedure.)

CAUSALITY

Even if we have found a difference between our two samples and can conclude that there is a difference in the populations from which they were drawn, we cannot necessarily conclude that the service caused the difference. There may be explanations for the difference in outcome other than the differences in service received. The best way to reduce the probability that other factors are operating is to randomly assign cases to the two groups. If that is done (and if there is little attrition from the groups) the results of the inferential analysis described above may be taken as evidence for causal relationships between service and outcome. If randomization has not taken place, it is difficult to reach causal conclusions, although more complex statistical analysis may help explore such matters.

An Example of Experimental Research

An example of a group experiment is found in the article "Social Work with Mental Patients in the Community" by Geraldine M. Koonce.[1] For many years an important policy direction in several social welfare areas has been that of deinstitutionalization. In the area of mental health, the large state psychiatric hospitals have been substantially reduced in size. The discharge of large numbers of chronically ill psychiatric patients to the community has resulted in substantial problems. Services for such patients in the community are often sparse and many are unable to maintain themselves outside the institution. Hence reinstitutionalization rates are high. The study cited above describes a program to prevent institutionalization of persons who were in danger of becoming chronic patients. Sixty-one patients who had been hospitalized between three and eighteen months were randomly assigned to one of three groups:

1. *Community treatment group.* These patients were discharged to the community and received extensive help with housing, job training and job finding, leisure time activities, and other supports. Nearly all patients were unmarried and were encouraged to separate themselves from their parental families.
2. *In-patient research control group.* The focus of this unit was on the reduction of symptoms and on teaching patients how to live in the community. Traditional therapeutic casework was provided including work with patients and their families, discharge planning, and referrals to community agencies.
3. *Other unit control group.* These patients remained on the wards they were on when selected for the study and received no special services.

After five months of the study the living arrangements and employment situation of the patients were assessed. All except one of the community treatment group were living in the community at that time (the one was in the hospital), while nine of the twenty other unit control group and four of the research unit control group were in the hospital. Results for employment situation were similarily in favor of the community treatment group.

Although the numbers of cases were small, the research does suggest that a community oriented rehabilitation program with extensive supports may be effective in maintaining at least some seriously ill patients in the community. The article promises further follow-up of these patients later on. The results of such a follow-up would be very useful in reaching more definitive conclusions. The fact that random assignment was used makes it less likely that the differences in outcome were due to differences in the patients before the intervention began. One criticism that might be made of the study is that the same social worker worked with both the community treatment group and the research unit control group. This seems to control for the social worker (that is, we can not claim that the differences in outcome were because of differences in social workers), but it is possible that the worker had more investment in the community group and that the results reflect this investment.

RESEARCH UTILIZATION

In an applied field, research must obviously be used if it is to be worthwhile. It has become commonplace to observe that human service professionals make very little use of the vast body of social science research. The reasons for this are many and in fact have been the subject of considerable research.

There is insufficient communication between practitioners and researchers. Practitioners believe that researchers investigate unimportant problems, ignoring the big issues in practice. In addition, they accuse researchers of talking in academic tongues, using language and terminology unfamiliar to practice. Researchers fault practitioners for being too action oriented and unwilling to engage in the intellectual work needed to adapt research findings to the needs of practice.

In recent years there has been developing interest in the problems of research utilization. Studies have been undertaken of the ways in which knowledge is disseminated and of the conditions under which research is utilized.

One of the most interesting developments in the area of the utilization of knowledge is the idea of *social research and development (social R and D).* Developers of this idea begin with the observation that there is a gap between the findings of research and the specification of practice principles. Practice principles cannot be derived directly from social science research. In the physical sciences a large cadre of engineers and applied scientists develop the findings of basic research into technology and eventually into products which are widely distributed. Advocates of social R and D seek to make use of the engineering paradigm and ideas from industrial R and D to develop social technologies. The purpose of social R and D is not to develop knowledge per se but programs and processes that can be used in dealing with social problems.

The core of most writing about R and D is the identification of a series of steps which lead to tested solutions and their adoption in practice. We will discuss here the steps suggested by two authors, Jack Rothman and Edwin Thomas.

Social R and D Rothman's social R and D model consists of six material stages connected by five operational steps.[2] The *material* stages consist of products such as generalizations, manuals, or the outcomes of field testing. The *operational* steps are the activities needed to produce the products. At any stage the developer may decide to return to earlier steps to refine the products.

The model begins with a social goal or problem. The first material stage is the existing pool of social science empirical knowledge. This knowledge is contained in books, journals, agency reports, dissertations, indexes, abstracts, and computerized data banks. The first operational step is retrieval of that knowledge relevant to the goal or problem and its codification into generalizations. The second material stage then is consensus findings, generalizations, and propositions. Generalizations can be made when there is agreement among the findings of various studies with few conflicting findings (a consensus of the studies).

The second operational step is conversion and design. In this step translations are made from the findings of science into concepts that can be used in practice, translations from description to prescription. The reality of the practice situation is considered in this step in terms of feasibility, cost, and other limitations. The outcome of this step is material stage three, application concepts. These concepts are still relatively abstract and need to be specified further before implementation.

Operational step three is initial operationalization and pilot testing. This involves specification of "locations, contexts, materials, resources, and behaviors for implementation." In this step practitioners engage in initial pilot testing of activities. This results in material stage four, application concepts in delimited form, an "operationalized statement of implementation in which resources and procedures are specified."

Next is operational step four, main field testing. Procedures are tried out on a broader scale with a range of situations and individuals. Careful evaluation accompanies this step, although it is directed at refining the procedures rather than at the acceptance or rejection of whole programs. Ways of dealing with problems of implementation in real life situations are developed. Often modifications of procedures are suggested, and it may be necessary to cycle back to pilot testing of these changes. Field testing results in material stage five, tested application concepts and the means to disseminate the concepts. These means include handbooks or manuals for practitioners as well as other media.

Operational step five is production and wide diffusion. This involves the mass production of the media for dissemination. It also involves the identification of potential users and the development of ways to reach them through promotional campaigns, workshops, consultation, training, and so forth. If all has gone well, this step should result in material stage six, broad practice use.

Developmental Research. The developmental research and utilization framework of Edwin Thomas has many similarities to Rothman's social R and D.[3] It is also directed at the development of social technology. It includes five main phases: analysis, development, evaluation, diffusion, and adoption. These phases are divided into fifteen operational steps. Some of these operational steps result in material conditions similar to Rothman's material stages.

Thomas' framework differs in important ways from the R and D model. Thomas views the analysis phase as being broader than research. Information from sources other than empirical findings should be sought, including practice experience, technology in other fields, and legal policy. The analysis phase should also include an assessment of the feasibility of technological development: Does it appear that the desired technology can be developed with acceptable cost?

In the development phase, Thomas suggests a number of procedures for the generation of innovations besides the use of existing empirical findings. Technological transfer consists of finding new ways of using existing technology. Novel application involves using the methods of an allied field. Experiential synthesis involves the generation out of practice experience of a new procedure, without reliance on research.

In contrast to Rothman, Thomas emphasizes the importance

of evaluation as a separate phase which includes trial use, field implementation, and revision or redesign, a process that may be repeated several times before the innovation is satisfactorily perfected.

Summary

In this chapter we introduced research methods involving the study of groups of individuals and considered the use of these methods in the evaluation of programs. Again as in single case studies the process of specification of objectives and intervention is critical. This leads to the design for the study and the procedures used to measure the variables of interest.

To arrive at definitive conclusions about the effectiveness of a program we must compare persons who experience the program with persons who do not. For the sake of sound conclusions, it is desirable that persons be assigned randomly to these conditions. Without this method, control of alternative explanations for the outcome must depend on statistical analysis.

The designs discussed in this chapter include the simple two group experimental-control design in which measurements are taken only after intervention, the before-after design, matched pairs designs, and designs utilizing more than two groups.

Issues in the analysis of data from group designs were introduced. These include the description of relationships between variables and the drawing of inferences about the population from which the subjects of the study were drawn. The chapter concludes with a consideration of new approaches to research utilization and the development of social technology.

Notes

1. Geraldine M. Koonce, Social Work with Mental Patients in the Community, *Social Work, 18*(3):30-34, 1973
2. Jack Rothman, *Social R & D: Research and Development in the Human Services,* Englewood Cliffs, N. J.: Prentice-Hall, 1980.
3. Edwin J. Thomas, Developmental Research: A Model for Interven-

tional Innovation, in Richard M. Grinnell, *Social Work Research and Evaluation*, Itasca, Il.: F. E. Peacock, 1981.

Bibliography

Material on the methodology of evaluative research is found in the bibliography for Chapter 2 and in the following:

Clark C. Abt, Ed. *The Evaluation of Social Programs*, Beverly Hills, Ca.: Sage Publications, 1976.

Donald T. Campbell and Julian C. Stanley, *Experimental and Quasi Experimental Designs for Research*, Chicago: Rand McNally, 1966.

Evaluation Studies Review Annual, published annually since 1976, Beverly Hills, Ca.: Sage Publications.

Peter H. Rossi, *Evaluation: A Systematic Approach*, Beverly Hills, Ca.: Sage Publications, 1979.

Peter H. Rossi and Walter Williams, Eds., *Evaluating Social Programs*, New York: Seminar Press, 1972.

Elmer L. Struening and Marcia Guttentag, *Handbook of Evaluation Research*, 2 vols., Beverly Hills, Ca.: Sage Publications, 1975.

Edward A. Suchman, *Evaluative Research*, New York: Russell Sage Foundation, 1967.

Carol H. Weiss, *Evaluating Action Programs*, Boston: Allyn and Bacon, 1972.

Carol H. Weiss, *Evaluation Research: Methods of Assessing Program Effectiveness*, Englewood Cliffs, N. J.: Prentice-Hall, 1972.

Surveys of evaluation research include the following:

Allen E. Bergin and Sol L. Garfield, *Handbook of Psychotherapy and Behavior Change*, New York: Wiley, 1st ed. 1971, 2nd. ed. 1978.

Joel Fischer, *The Effectiveness of Social Casework*, Springfield, Il.: Charles C. Thomas, 1976.

Gene V. Glass, Barry McGaw, and Mary Lee Smith, *Meta-Analysis in Social Research*, Beverly Hills, Ca.: Sage Publications, 1981.

Arnold P. Goldstein and Sanford J. Dean, *The Investigation of Psychotherapy*, New York: Wiley, 1966.

Alan S. Gurman and Andrew M. Razin, Eds. *Effective Psychotherapy: A Handbook of Research*, New York: Pergamon Press, 1977.

Julian Meltzoff and Melvin Kornreich, *Research in Psychotherapy*, New York: Atherton, 1970.

Edward J. Mullen, James R. Dumpson and associates, *Evaluation of Social Intervention*, San Francisco: Jossey Bass, 1972.

Mary Lee Smith, Gene V. Glass, and Thomas I. Miller, *The Benefits of Psychotherapy*, Baltimore: Johns Hopkins University Press, 1980.

Gary E. Stollak, Bernard G. Guerney, Jr., and Meyer Rothberg, Eds., *Psychotherapy Research*, Chicago: Rand McNally, 1966.

Katherine M. Wood, Casework Effectiveness: A New Look at the Evidence, *Social Work*, 23(6):437-458, 1978.

Journals

Evaluation

Evaluation and Program Planning

Evaluation Review formerly *Evaluation Quarterly*

Development and Change

Knowledge Evaluation and the Health Professions

5

Research on People and their Problems

This chapter covers two types of studies: needs assessment and research on the origins and dynamics of people's problems.

Needs Assessment Research

What today is called *needs assessment research* is perhaps the oldest form of social work research. It had its origins in the great social surveys and fact-finding efforts of the social reformers of the nineteenth and early twentieth centuries. As early as the 1700s John Howard counted men held in jails in Britain and Europe and described the conditions of their incarceration. His work was intended to bring about reform of prisons. In the 1840s Dorothea Dix set out to document the numbers and living conditions of mentally ill persons in the United States, an effort which culminated in the development of huge state hospital systems. In England Charles Booth engaged in extensive surveys of the life of the poor in East London and published his seventeen volume work

The Life and Labor of the People of London (1902-1903). Another massive study was the Pittsburgh Survey (1909-1914), an investigation of the effects of industrialization in a modern city.

Needs assessment research is also related to epidemiological research, the study of the extent and distribution of various disorders in society. In medicine this kind of research has helped to conquer a number of infectious diseases. In the 1950s and 1960s several large epidemiological studies were made of the prevalance of mental illness in various communities, studies which helped us understand the relationships between social factors and mental disorder.[1]

By needs assessment research we mean research aimed at documenting the needs of people living within a particular community or other geographical region or the needs of a particular subgroup within a region. For example, we may be interested in detailing the needs of a particular low income community or of the aged population within a city. Needs assessment surveys are carried out by welfare councils, funding organizations, planning bodies, or social agencies interested in planning services for a particular area.

Needs assessment studies are primarily descriptive in nature, although they may occasionally suggest causal relationships among phenomena. It may seem that formulating the research question is straightforward: We want to determine the problems and needs of a particular group of people. However, this is tantamount to asking for a complete description of a community, since it is desirable to know a community's strengths as well as its weaknesses in order to know how to approach its problems most effectively. To provide a complete description of even a small community is impossible. Hence a needs assessment study requires a more specific focus: the problems of particular groups (for example, youth) or of people in particular locations (for example, housing).

In the process of formulating the research question, it is helpful to make use of two sources of information: community residents and available data on the community. A considerable understanding of the area can be gained from the study of available information—census data, police statistics, and figures from health, zoning, and building departments. The reliability and current validity of each must be assessed. For example, census data may be out of date and crime statistics vary in their completeness, even within a single city. Nonetheless, a beginning picture of the characteristics and problems of a community may be derived from such data.

Residents, in particular community leaders and others with insights into the nature of the community, are important contributors to the formulation of needs assessment studies. The views of such persons naturally differ; they see different things in the community and have differing stakes. It is important to get several divergent viewpoints. Of course, involving important community figures in the formulation and execution of the study is also valuable in that it makes it more likely that the results will be used later on.

Needs assessment studies are usually surveys involving interviews or written questionnaires administered to samples of community residents. Hence the principal design problems are those of questionnaire construction and sampling.

QUESTIONNAIRE CONSTRUCTION

Details of the process of questionnaire construction are dealt with in Chapter 10, so we will consider here only those aspects of particular relevance to needs assessment studies. The process of formulation of the research questions should result in specification of particular areas to be covered by the questionnaire. From this list specific questions are drafted. As with most questionnaires, the instrument should include both structured and open-ended questions. The structured (perhaps fixed-response) questions assure that certain areas are adequately covered and that uniform data is obtained from all respondents, while the open-ended questions allow for the discovery of problems and perspectives not anticipated by the researcher at the outset.

In a community with divergent cultural backgrounds and educational attainments it is important to pay particular attention to the wording of questions. Questions should be worded as simply and clearly as possible and should avoid abstractions which might be misunderstood. It may be useful for the questionnaire to make use of local colloquialisms. *Leading questions*, that is, questions that suggest correct answers should be avoided as should questions that might be embarrassing or require skills or capacities respondents might not have. Sometimes difficult areas can be approached with *projective* questions. For example, rather than asking a teenager directly whether he has ever been in trouble, a question about most kids in the neighborhood might be asked. It must be kept in mind that projective questions often have low validity. In a bilingual neighborhood it may be necessary to translate the questionnaire or to use bilingual interviewers.

SAMPLING

Often it is not possible to interview all of the relevant population, and a sample is necessary. Since the objective is to develop a picture of the population that is as accurate as possible, the construction of the sample is particularly critical. The sample should be *probabilistic*, that is, all members of the population should have a specified probability of selection into the sample. Sometimes this is achieved by taking a simple random sample, selecting randomly from a list of all possible respondents. Alternatively, sampling may be done in stages, for example, taking a random sample of blocks within the community and selecting respondents randomly from each block. Often it is desirable to use more elaborate sampling schemes.

The results of a study using a sample are only estimates of the characteristics of the population. These will not be exactly the same as the population values; the aim, of course, is to assure as close a likeness as possible. In general, the larger the sample size the closer the sample estimates will be to the population values. However, sample sizes are usually limited by available resources and time. Statisticians are able to estimate the accuracy of results from a certain size sample. Conversely, it is possible to estimate the size of a sample required to obtain a certain level of accuracy.

Sometimes it is possible to construct a sample in such a way that the estimates are more efficient, that is, so that they are more likely to be close to the real value. This is done by employing more complex procedures than simple random sampling. Researchers may need to consult with sampling experts to figure out how to do this.

An Example of Needs Assessment

In recent years the deinstitutionalization of the mentally ill has been a significant trend in many states. Persons confined for many years in large state psychiatric hospitals have been released in great numbers. In the early 1970s legislation was enacted in Florida which encouraged the release of patients from the state hospital. A study was undertaken of patients in the hospital from an eight county area to determine their characteristics, the kinds of services they would be likely to require if released to the community, and the services actually available in the community.[2]

Data on patients were obtained from hospital records, questionnaires filled out by hospital personnel, and where possible, interviews with patients.

A total of 369 patients were involved in the study; 75 percent had been hospitalized for more than three years. It was found that a large proportion of patients needed considerable supervision and would not be able to live outside the hospital without extensive supportive services. Many would require nursing-home care and others would need supervision of medication. Few could be expected to work. It was found that resources in the community were woefully inadequate to provide the needed care. The few nursing homes in the area were already full. The mental health center and county departments of public health were already strained. It was clear therefore that the release of significant numbers of these patients would result in "insurmountable hardships for patients as well as for service personnel in the . . . area."

Research on the Origins and Dynamics of People's Problems

How people come to grief and what maintains or mitigates their troubles is a vast area of study involving many disciplines and points of view. Findings potentially useful to the human service practitioner come from a wide variety of sources: from sociology, research on the origins and dynamics of broad social problems, on organizational functioning and malfunctioning; from economics, research on the allocation of resources and what can go wrong in that allocation; from social psychology, research on the effects of groups and communication on individual behavior; from developmental psychology, research on normal and pathological human development; and from psychiatry and psychoanalysis, research on the inner workings of the mind. Studies on the normal functioning of organizations, groups, and individuals is useful in understanding what goes wrong and what to do about it.

Although research in these areas has traditionally been the province of academic disciplines, workers in the human service professions are becoming more and more involved in such studies. In their work they have easy access to much data on human behavior, while the academic researcher usually must work with people outside the university to gather his data. Except at the extremes, it is difficult to define the proper perview of the researcher in the professions as opposed to that of an academic scientist. The situation is clouded further by the fact that academic disciplines are turning more and more to investigate applied issues. That is, psychologists and sociologists are increasingly studying problems of people in real life instead of conducting experiments in laboratories.

Few generalizations are possible about this wide range of research concerns, but some comments can be made. Research on the origins and dynamics of people's problems is usually associational rather than experimental in nature. It is not possible, for ethical and other reasons, to experimentally manipulate the conditions of people's lives such that pathology or other disorder might arise. Hence the study of the development of individuals, groups, or organizations must depend on relatively passive observation, often over some period of time. The investigation of pathology usually rests on the study of persons who already have the problem. Often this involves trying to reconstruct the past and making comparisons with persons who do not have the problem.

In such research we seek associations which we think indicate causal connections between variables and events. For example, we might observe that children whose mothers are emotionally distant are more likely to develop psychological problems than those whose mothers are warm and close. We are led to conclude that the mother's emotional tone causes or at least contributes to the psychological well-being of the child.

As indicated previously, attempting to draw causal connections on the basis of associations among variables is fraught with difficulties arising from the availability of alternative explanations. First, it is possible that the direction of causality is backwards; perhaps it is the child's difficult behavior that causes the mother to be distant rather than the other way around. Second, it is possible that another variable is the cause of the association; perhaps factors in the environment of the family cause the mother to be distant and also cause the child to develop psychological problems.

There are two main ways of trying to control for possible alternative explanations in this situation, neither of them foolproof. One is to track phenomena over some period of time, taking measurements of variables at several points to determine exactly when changes take place. If the child appears normal at first, then later becomes disturbed, while the mother is emotionally distant throughout, it seems unlikely that the child's behavior caused the mother's distance. The second method of control involves measuring variables representing all the other possible explanations for an observed association and then attempting, through the analysis of data, to assess their likelihood. For example, we would try to think of and measure other factors that might cause psychological problems in children. The possibility that the other factors are important can then be checked in the data analysis.

An additional problem with research on the origins and dynamics of people's problems is that a particular phenomenon may have different causes in different situations. For example, depression has many causes. It may result from psychological, social, or physiological influences. Then too, particular events may have many different outcomes. The child of a distant mother may become psychotic or delinquent, in response to other factors.

The design of studies on the origins of pathology is usually either longitudinal or cross-sectional. Sometimes these studies have comparison groups of persons not suffering from the disorder. Except in the psychoanalytic literature, few such studies are of single cases. In general, designs are stronger (their conclusions are more convincing) if they are longitudinal and if they compare people that suffer from the disorder with others who do not. There are many examples of ingenious designs, for example, the comparison of twins one of whom suffers from a disorder while the other does not.

A Study of Empathy, Stress, and Child Abuse

An example of research on the origins of problems is reported by Charlene Letourneau.[3] Much research on child abuse has focused on the hypothesis that abuse is related to the level of stress experienced by the parent. Some programs for abusive parents emphasize this explanation through the provision of crisis intervention services. In this study, that hypothesis was compared to the hypothesis that the empathy level of the parent is associated with child abuse; that is, parents with low empathy are more likely to abuse their children.

The study design involved the comparison of a group of abusive mothers with a group of mothers who were not abusive (so far as was known). There were thirty mothers in each group. The groups were similar on such variables as income, race, social class, education, family structure, age, and number of children. The study of groups that were relatively homogeneous on such variables reduces the possibility that those variables could account for any relationship between empathy and child abuse.

Empathy was operationalized by two tests which were administered to all sixty subjects. These tests were paper and pencil instruments which had been developed in other research. One of them conceptualized empathy in terms of the ability of the individual to take the role of the other. The other test defined empathy as a vicarious emotional response to the perceived emotional experiences of others. The reliability and validity of these tests had been explored in earlier studies.

A third measure consisted of a series of role plays to determine maternal responsiveness. Although the author does not make it clear, this apparently was thought of as another aspect of empathy. The mothers were presented with situations in which a child seeks comfort or help, or becomes angry. The situations were presented by means of the recorded voice of a child. The respondent was then asked what she would do. The responses were coded on four scales: (1) help-withholding, (2) comfort-with-holding, (3) sensitivity to the child's needs, and (4) aggression. The reliability of this coding was checked by having some of the ratings done by two people.

The measure of stress was a listing of forty-three potentially stressful events. Subjects checked the events they had experienced in the past year.

Statistical analysis consisted of comparisons of the average score for each scale recorded for abusive mothers with that recorded for nonabusive mothers. Abusive mothers were found to have lower average scores on the measures of empathy and maternal responsiveness. However, the groups did not differ on the measure of degree of stress experienced. The study results suggest that degree of empathy and maternal responsiveness may be more important than stress in explaining child abuse. The author is properly cautious in reaching conclusions, however, pointing out that the measure of stress only counts potentially stressful events, without accounting for individual responses to them. In addition, the measure does not take into account positive events or mitigating factors (such as the amount of support available from others in overcoming the effects of negative events).

Despite its limitations, the study is a useful contribution to our understanding of a serious social problem. It also points the way to additional research.

Summary

In this chapter we have considered needs assessment research and research on the origins and dynamics of people's problems. Needs assessment studies are primarily descriptive and are designed to assist in planning services for a community or a group. Usually, the principal source of data about needs comes from people in the community or group, hence, sampling and questionnaire construction deserve careful attention. Often these studies are accompanied by surveys of resources available to meet needs.

Research on the origins and dynamics of people's problems covers a very wide area of concern to many academic disciplines and professions. In such research, groups of people or other social systems are studied. It is infrequent that controlled experimental designs are used in such studies, instead passive observation of the associations among variables is employed. Often this type of research involves comparing persons with certain problems with persons who are not experiencing those problems. Longitudinal designs and data analysis are used to control for alternative explanations for the development of the problem.

Notes

1. See August B. Hollingshead and Frederick C. Redlich, *Social Class and Mental Illness*, New York: Wiley, 1958 and Jerome K. Myers and Bertram H. Roberts *Family and Class Dynamics in Mental Illness*, New York: Wiley, 1959 for a study conducted in New Haven, Connecticut. A study conducted in midtown Manhatten is Leo Srole, et al. *Mental Health in the Metropolis*, New York: McGraw Hill, 1962. The three volume Stirling County Study authored by Alexander Leighton and his colleagues concerns research carried out in Nova Scotia. The books are (all published by Basic Books, New York): Volume one: Alexander Leighton, *My Name is Legion*, 1959, Volume two: Charles C. Hughes et al., *People of Cove and Woodlot*, 1960 and Volume three: Dorothea C. Leighton et al., *The Character of Danger*, 1963.

2. Leila Calhoun Deasy and Carolyn I. Steele, An Analysis of a State Hospital Population Subject to Release Under Florida Law, *Hospital and Community Psychiatry*, 27(1):42-44, 1976.

3. Empathy and Stress: How they affect parental aggression, *Social Work*, 26(5):383-389, 1981.

6

Research on Human
Interaction

In this chapter we consider research into the nature of interactions among people. Included here is research on the processes of treatment, studies of family interaction, and studies of interactions among other individuals. These areas of investigation all have considerable methodological similarities.

The questions asked in such studies are largely descriptive or associational in nature. For example, we might want to describe the nature of psychotherapeutic interaction or to find out whether families of schizophrenic children interact in different ways from families of normal children. The extent to which theory governs the questions asked varies considerably. Sometimes the studies are exploratory, seeking merely to describe the complexities of a certain type of interaction. Other studies are designed to test well-formulated hypotheses concerning interaction. Examples of the latter are studies of the *double bind* hypothesis on the origin of schizophrenia, the theory that parents of a schizophrenic child more often submit the child to messages that conflict at different levels of communication than do parents of normal children.

If we want to understand how people interact with each other we will need to begin with records of interactions. Questionnaires are very limited in their usefulness for the study of interaction. People cannot tell us about the most interesting aspects of communication since the events in an interaction often occur rapidly and much communication behavior is not conscious. Studies of interaction by clinicians are also suspect for the same reasons. Often we want to study interaction that is as natural as possible, so it is difficult to study it in a structured experimental situation.

At one time so-called process recordings, written accounts from memory of treatment interactions were used, but these have proven to be too unreliable for most research purposes. Today the record is most often an electronic recording, either audiotape or videotape, from which categories of the events that occur are developed. The analysis of the interaction is often aided by having available a written transcript of the words spoken.

Many different aspects of interaction have been examined in such studies. Some researchers put emphasis on the formal or process aspects of communication, while others emphasize the content of interaction, that is, the meanings of the words spoken. The aspects of communication that have been studied can be categorized as follows:

1. The words, phrases or sentences spoken. Coding schemes for words, phrases, or sentences vary in the extent to which the meanings of the verbalizations are inferred. At one extreme, only the manifest content of the words is coded; for example, words might be coded as to whether they refer to the speaker (words like I, me, mine), to other people, or neither. Another example is the coding of a sentence as a statement, a command, or a question. At the other extreme, coding schemes may involve a great deal of inference on the part of coders as to the meaning of verbalizations. For example, Florence Hollis developed a coding scheme for casework procedures which included categories for the following activities: sustaining, direct influence, catharsis or ventilation, and reflective consideration of a number of areas.[1] Of course at both extremes inferences as to meanings are made but when only manifest content is coded, these inferences are made in the stage of data analysis rather than in the coding stage. For example, a lot of refer-

ences to the self might be taken as indicating something about the individual's personality characteristics.

2. Other aspects of the verbalizations (called *paralinguistic* characteristics) such as tone of voice, pitch, inflection, tempo, and stress. Sometimes coding schemes for these aspects of verbal behavior are used without paying any attention to the content of the speech.

3. Nonverbal behavior such as posture, gestures and direction of gaze (sometimes called *kinesics*).

The initial raw data in the form of audio or video recordings are first reduced to a set of marks on paper representing events that occurred during the interaction. A number of problems arise in this process.

As indicated above, the verbal and nonverbal types of behaviors to be coded, must be identified. The types of events become the variables of the study, and this stage corresponds to the selection of relevant variables in other studies. Since it is impossible to capture everything that goes on in an interaction, some selection must be made.

After the types of behaviors are established, categories within them must be determined. Here the problem is the fineness of the categories; for example, should the researcher code only whether or not a person moves his hand or also how he moves it and what he touches?

The level of abstraction to be used in the initial coding is crucial to the identification of variables and the determination of coding categories. As indicated above, some variables require a great deal of judgment on the part of coders, for example, the determination of whether or not a double-bind has occurred. At the other extreme are variables that are very concrete, involving little judgment, for example, inflection of voice or moment to moment hand movement.

Advocates of coding categories that are at a low level of abstraction argue that they are more reliable and precise and thus provide a sounder base for developing an understanding of interaction. In their view, allowing judgment to enter the coding process results in the data being skewed by theoretical preconceptions. In addition, much of importance in the interaction may be missed in coding schemes that require a high level of inference, since what is observed must be fit into theoretically based categories. In opposition to this view, it is argued that it is not possible, or if theoretically possible, not feasible, to build up from such concrete categories to levels of understanding that are important. The issue of meaning has importance here. Advocates of concrete coding avoid consideration of the meaning of interaction events to the participants on the grounds that it is impossible to determine this factor reliably. However, it is in the meaning of events to people that their impact on those involved is to be found. Hence it seems difficult to avoid meanings entirely.

Closely connected with the level of abstraction is the size of the unit of interaction to be coded. For example, one could code an encounter as a whole, speeches within interactions, sentences, phrases, words, or syllables. Some investigators have even coded individual frames in motion pictures of interactions. After one determines the unit of interaction to be employed it is often necessary to unitize the interaction; that is, one must go through the recording (or perhaps a written transcript of it) and specify where each unit begins and ends.

Questions of sampling are often important in interactional research. The process of coding is time consuming and expensive and becomes more so the more microscopic the analysis. Hence often only a few, relatively short, interaction segments constitute the data for an entire study. In this situation random selection may not be the best way to choose the interactions to be examined. Rather, interactions most likely to be informative are selected.

DATA REDUCTION AND ANALYSIS

The result of the coding stage of interaction research is a series of marks on pages representing the categorization of behaviors occurring within an interaction. Further steps must be taken to make these marks meaningful.

At one time, analytic techniques used in interaction analysis were relatively simple. Counts of various kinds of behaviors were made and interpretations rested on them. Comparisons of the frequencies of behavior categories were then made. The two studies described at the end of this chapter utilized such analyses.

More recently it has been recognized that much of the richness of interactional data lies in their sequential nature, that is, the order in which events occur. As a result efforts have been made to find analytic techniques that preserve and take into account the order of behaviors. These techniques have as their objective the detection of patterns or regularities in the interaction. Sometimes researchers begin with well-formulated hypotheses about such patterns. Other investigators develop hypotheses about regularities by scanning the coding sheets of interactions. For example, it might be noted that when a client is asked a question about himself he shows signs of anxiety (in the form of accelerated speech, movement of the body, and so forth). Once these hypotheses are developed they are systematically investigated. That is, we would find every instance in which the client was asked a question about himself and see whether or not it was followed by signs of anxiety.

INTERACTION PROCESS ANALYSIS

One of the first schemes for the analysis of interaction was Interaction Process Analysis (IPA) developed by Robert Bales. IPA was designed for the study of interaction in groups and is based on certain theoretical notions about the activities that generally occur in groups. These activities are thought of as either instrumental or expressive. *Instrumental activities* are directed at helping the group accomplish its task, for example, solving some problem. *Expressive activities* are directed at maintaining or altering group feelings, climate, or cohesion. The IPA has twelve categories of acts (communications involving single phrases with a subject and predicate). Examples of these are seems friendly, gives suggestion, and asks for opinion.[2]

SIMULATION AND ANALOG STUDIES

The *analog* technique provides another procedure for the investigation of therapeutic intervention. An analog simulates the interview situation to see what a practitioner will do under certain circumstances. Practitioners are given practice situations either in writing, on video or audio tape, or by means of a live actor. The situation may be derived from real life or contrived. The practitioner is asked to respond in the way he would in actual practice. In some studies, recordings of entire interviews are presented to workers. The recording is stopped after each client speech to determine the practitioner's response. Responses are then coded and analyzed.

Analog procedures are useful when it is not feasible or desirable to investigate therapeutic interventions through the examination of real interactions. They are particularly useful when it is desirable to standardize the stimuli presented to practitioners. For example if one wanted to determine the real differences (rather than the theoretical differences) in the approach of practitioners of varying theoretical persuasions one might present the same case to several therapists in an analog design. The technique can also be used to determine the effects of contextual factors on therapists' behavior. For example the effects of social class could be determined by presenting the same case to a group of practitioners. Half of the respondents might be told that the case involves a poor family while the other half would be told that the case is a middle class family. Differences, if any, in the way the two groups of practitioners handled the case could then be examined.

Analog studies are limited in that the exact conditions of therapeutic intervention cannot be duplicated. It is also likely that the therapist in an analog situation will not behave exactly as he or she would in real life. Nonetheless, analog studies have proven useful for investigating certain aspects of therapeutic process. Some investigators have even used computers to engage in these studies, writing computer programs which respond in ways similar to clients. Practitioners then communicate with the client-program by means of a computer terminal.

Family Processes and Schizophrenia

An example of a study of family interaction is reported in the book *Interaction in Families: An Experimental Study of Family Processes and Schizophrenia*.[3] This is a very extensive study involving a complex design. Samples of interaction among two parents and a child were recorded and coded on a number of dimensions. The design provided for several comparisons:

1. Families with a schizophrenic child versus normal families.
2. Schizophrenics with good premorbid histories versus schizophrenics with poor premorbid histories. Good premorbid history means a person who became ill suddenly, with few indications of previous serious psychiatric problems, while poor premorbid history means a person with previous indications of difficulties.
3. Families with male patients versus those with female patients.
4. Interactions of parents with a schizophrenic child versus interactions of the same parents with a well child of the same sex.

The study was designed to provide evidence regarding a number of theories about the relationship between family interaction and the development and course of schizophrenia. For example, the theory of *pseudo-mutuality* suggests that interaction in families of schizophrenics is characterized by expressions of support and agreement that are not genuine.[4] Another example is the double bind hypothesis mentioned earlier, the suggestion that schizophrenics experience messages from their parents that are conflicting at different levels of communication (for example, the content and affective tone of the message may be in conflict).[5]

The researchers used the *revealed differences* technique of Strodbeck.[6] The parents and child separately completed a paper and pencil instrument which presented thirty-eight situations involving interpersonal difficulties. The respondent was asked what should be done in these situations. The situations on which the family members disagreed were identified, and they were asked to discuss these situations and see if they could come to an agreement. Discussions were tape recorded and usually lasted less than an hour. The particular items on which subjects disagreed did not matter, they were merely used to provide a more or less standard stimulus for a discussion.

Transcripts of the recordings were then made and divided into units of interaction, ideally consisting of a single sentence or a phrase with a single subject and single predicate. However, a complicated set of rules had to be developed for the unitizing operation, since natural speech is often ungrammatical and incomplete.

Each unit was then coded in a large number of ways. Examples of codes were who was speaking to whom, affect (positive, negative, or neutral and whether the affect was linked to a relationship), and interruptions. Coders were carefully trained and reliability was checked periodically during the long process of coding. For most of the codes percentage of agreement between two coders was above 85 percent.

From the codes for the individual acts, a series of interaction indices were computed for each family session. *Interaction indices* are proportions of interaction units that fall into various categories. Sometimes the denominator used for the proportion was the total number of units in the session, at other times it was some relevant subtotal. Examples of interaction indices are proportions of positive and negative affect.

A wide range of findings concerning interaction differences among types of families were reported. It is not possible to summarize these findings in detail here, but a couple of examples will be given. It was found that normal families were more expressive and their affect was more positive than schizophrenic families. Further (contrary to expectations), it was found that families in which the schizophrenic had a good premorbid history had the most negative affect.

Patient-Therapist Interaction

In the book *Patterns in Human Interaction*, Henry L. Lennard and Arnold Bernstein describe a series of investigations into both family and therapeutic interactions.[7] We describe here the study of patient-therapist interactions. Tape recordings were made of many therapeutic sessions involving patients with varying diagnoses at different stages of treatment. The interactions were unitized in a way very similar to that of the previous study. A unit was a "*Proposition*, defined as a verbalization containing a subject and predicate, whether expressed or implied."[8] Units were then categorized, depending on the focus of the study.

One of the topics studied by Lennard and Bernstein was the process of *role induction* in psychotherapy, that is, the ways in which patient and therapist determine the rules that govern their interaction. Role induction takes place in part through explicit *primary role system communication* which consists of questions from the patient about what he should say or do in the sessions and statements by the therapist about what is expected of the patient and what the therapist will do. Role induction also includes discussion of such things as fees and appointment times. The authors found, not unexpectedly, that such communications were more frequent early in treatment than later. However, rather interestingly, they also found that primary role system communications were much less prevalent in work with schizophrenics than with neurotic patients. Schizophrenic patients very rarely asked questions about the rules of the game. The authors suggest that this may reflect the etiology of schizophrenia and that it indicates one of the reasons the disorder is so difficult to treat. *They do not assume the patient role.* That is to say, they do not accept the conditions and limitations of the treatment relationship. They appear to suffer from a general inability to differentiate among role relationships and to behave in accordance with the specific expectations that varied social situations require.[9]

Summary

In this chapter we have discussed research on human interaction. The procedures are primarily applied by human service professionals to the study of family interaction, therapeutic processes, treatment group processes, and work group interactions. These studies begin with recordings of sample interactions. The events in these interactions (for example, sentences, words, speeches, gestures, postures) are then classified and subjected to analysis to detect regularities or patterns. Many different categorizations of interactional events have been devised. These may be considered the variables of interactional research.

Issues in interactional research include the level of abstraction used in coding, the unitization of an interaction, sampling of interaction segments, and how codes of small events can be built up into more complex ideas. To be useful the analysis of interactional data should preserve the sequential nature of the events.

Analog and simulation studies are used primarily for the study of therapeutic processes. Professionals are put in situations which simulate the therapeutic encounter. They are asked to behave as they would in the real situation or to report how they would react. Simulation studies are particularly useful when it is desirable to standardize stimuli, as in the study of differences among practitioners or the study of how practitioners react to persons in different categories.

Notes

1. Florence Hollis, *Casework: A Psychosocial Therapy*, New York: Random House, 1964.
2. Robert Bales, *Interaction Process Analysis*, Reading, Ma.: Addison-Wesley, 1950; and *Personality and Interpersonal Behavior*, New York: Holt, Rinehart, and Winston, 1970.
3. Elliot G. Mishler and Nancy E. Waxler, *Interaction in Families: An Experimental Study of Family Processes and Schizophrenia*, New York: Wiley, 1968.
4. L. C. Wynne, I. Ryckoff, J. Day, and S. Hirsch, Pseudomutuality in the Family Relations of Schizophrenics, *Psychiatry*, 21:205-220, 1958.
5. G. Bateson, D. D. Jackson, J. Haley, and J. Weakland, Toward a Theory of Schizophrenia, *Behavioral Science*, 1:251-264, 1956.
6. Fred Strodbeck, Husband-wife Interaction over Revealed Differences, *American Sociological Review*, 16:468-473, 1951.
7. Henry L. Lennard and Arnold Bernstein, *Patterns of Human Interaction*, San Francisco: Jossey-Bass, 1969.
8. *Ibid*, p. 57.
9. *Ibid*, p. 153.

Bibliography

Research on human interaction is discussed in:

Starkey Duncan and Donald W. Fiske, *Face to Face Interaction*, Hillsdale, N. J.: Lawrence Erlbaum Associates, 1977.

B. Glick and S. Gross, Marital Interaction and Marital Conflict: A Critical Evaluation of Current Research Strategies, *Journal of Marriage and the Family*, 37:505-512, 1975.

J. Gottman, *Marital Interaction: Experimental Investigations*, New York: Academic Press, 1979.

J. Haley, Critical Overview of Present Status of Family Interaction Research, in J. Framo, *Family Interaction: A Dialogue Between Family Researchers and Family Therapists*, New York: Springer, 1972.

J. Riskin and E. Faunce, Family Interaction Scales: I, II, III, *Archives of General Psychiatry*, 22:504-537, 1970.

J. Riskin and E. Faunce, An Evaluative Review of Family Interaction Research, *Family Process*, 11:365-455, 1972.

S. Weitz, Ed., *Nonverbal Communication*, New York: Oxford University Press, 1979.

William D. Winter and Antonio J. Ferreira, eds. *Research in Family Interaction*, Palo Alto, Ca.: Science and Behavior Books, 1969.

7

Qualitative Methods

Most of this book reflects a point of view about research that has constituted the dominant approach to social science during most of this century, an approach that has come to be called quantitative. In recent years, a number of new approaches to scientific methodology have been proposed, some of which we will describe in this chapter. These approaches were originally developed as a reaction against a model of science that some researchers thought was too constraining, limiting the kinds of problems that could be addressed. Much of the writing by advocates of these new methods is accompanied by philosophical discussions in which traditional methods are attacked and newer methods defended on epistemological grounds. Advocates believe that the old methods arose out of the philosophy of logical positivism, a point of view that has been roundly attacked by a number of modern philosophers.

Characteristics of the New Approaches

The most dominant characteristic of the newer methodologies is a naturalistic approach. In this view the researcher should try to

understand people and events on their own terms without impos-
ing his frame of reference on them. Preconceptions about what
will be found should be avoided. In concrete terms this means
the researcher should not use predetermined categories for the
data. Instead, unstructured observations should be made and categories and organizing principles should emerge from these observations rather than from previous theorizing.

Of course it is impossible to view the world with no preconceptions at all. Our previous experiences, knowledge, and values
will all have an effect on what we see and how we see it. Advocates of qualitative approaches attempt to make a virtue of that
fact, asserting that fully objective knowledge is impossible and
the researcher should accept the active role he has in shaping the
data.

Writers on qualitative methods have suggested that these approaches are also characterized by:

1. The effort to understand social events from the point of view
   of persons involved in them. Qualitative approaches emphasize this focus rather than that of explaining why things happen. One strives for *verstehen*, a deep understanding of human beings in which it is assumed that people should be
   understood in ways that objects cannot be understood.
2. Emphasis on the processes of social interaction rather than the
   outcomes. That is, qualitative methods stress description of
   the details of what happens instead of trying to measure the
   end result.
3. Orientation to the discovery of insights rather than to confirm-
   ing hypotheses. Qualitative inquiry usually does not begin
   with well-formulated hypotheses. Rather it tries to discover
   new patterns from which new hypotheses can be formulated.

None of these factors uniquely characterize qualitative methods, since quantitative inquiry can display them as well. There
are many quantitative studies which try to understand the internal point of view of individuals, which are process rather than
outcome oriented, and which strive to discover rather than confirm. Insofar as there are differences between quantitative and
qualitative methods in regard to these elements, they are only
differences in emphasis.

There are a number of approaches to qualitative inquiry which differ in focus. We will describe three of these.

Ethnomethodology

Ethnomethodology grew out of the methods developed by anthropologists for the study of primitive cultures. A researcher who wishes to understand a primitive culture must immerse himself in it. He must strive to gain the confidence of persons in the culture and to understand cultural phenomena from the standpoint of its members. This requires months and perhaps years of living with the people involved. A number of sociologists have adapted the techniques of anthropologists to the study of communities, organizations, and other social entities in our culture.

An important early step in ethnomethodological research is gaining entry to the social situation to be studied and the confidence of persons in it. The other participants in the system must accept the researcher and be willing to talk frankly and openly to him. The data in these studies come from observing social phenomena such as interactions among people and from in-depth unstructured interviews. The latter will not be successful unless those being studied are candid in their descriptions and assessments. A researcher who gains the full confidence of participants may also become emotionally involved with them; managing these involvements is a critical problem for the investigator. Being involved with one person or group may prevent him from seeing how other participants view the situation. This may even cause others to be suspicious and refuse to cooperate. Since different people view the same social situation in different ways, it is important that the researcher attempt to understand all points of view.

Ethnomethodology attempts to understand how people arrive at definitions of their situation and how they shape their view of reality. Interactions among people are critical in such processes, so the researcher examines them in great detail. In theory, interactions are structured by unspoken and often unconscious rules. For example, there are rules governing turn-taking, the process by which one person stops talking and another starts. Others specify how conversations should be started and ended. Rules differ from one situation to another; for example, one set governs conversations among close friends while another controls interactions among strangers. The ethnomethodologist attempts to understand these conversational structures.

Besides rules, which are largely unconscious, conversations between people who know each other are also characterized by many tacit understandings. Conversations are carried out in the context of shared definitions of the situation and of knowing each other's attitudes on a variety of subjects. In any conversation between people who know each other much goes without saying. Close friends do not have to finish sentences, the other knows what is coming. The researcher must try to identify these understandings.

An important tool for understanding interactions is the analysis of *indexical expressions,* words or phrases which are given specific meaning by the context in which they are used or the way they are said. An outside observer would not understand them correctly or would consider them to be ambiguous, but they have clear meanings to the participants in a conversation. Pronouns and words like here, there, now, and then are always indexical expressions since they require a context to be meaningful. However, nearly every other word or phrase could be indexical if it had a special meaning to the participants in a conversation.

The goal of the ethnomethodologist is not to determine what indexicals mean (although that might be done) but rather to determine the rules that participants in a conversation use to make sense of them. Discovering these rules will reveal much about how participants view the world.

The raw data of ethnomethodological research are recorded in field notes which are written as soon as possible after each encounter with the social situation being investigated. *Field notes* attempt to capture as much detail as possible of the conversations, interviews, and observations of the researcher. It is important to record not only what was said but how it was said and details of its context. Once the data collection is completed the research is written up in the form of an ethnography. The distillation of field notes and the preparation of the ethnography can take almost as long as the data collection itself. Out of the mass of details captured in the field notes the researcher must come to conclusions about regularities in interactions in this social system.

The process often involves sifting through many hypotheses about what really happened and why, then testing each hypothesis against the evidence in the notes. As in other forms of research, alternative explanations for what is observed must be considered and carefully assessed.

AN ETHNOMETHODOLOGICAL STUDY

An interesting example of the use of ethnomethodological procedures for the understanding of social problems is Reyes Ramos' study of a poor Mexican-American family in a small town in Colorado.[1] The family consisted of a mother and five boys ranging in age from eight to twenty. The oldest was in a state reformatory. Family difficulties had markedly increased with the death of the father a year and a half before the study was done. The mother had to work outside the home and was unable to provide much supervision for the children who did poorly in school and were frequently truant. The study revolved around a summons of the mother and two of the children to appear in court on a truancy petition initiated by the school. The author's purpose was to "...call attention to the background knowledge Mexican Americans use as interpretative schemes to cope with the problematic features in their daily lives, and the role Mexican Americans and their helpers play in producing the problematic features in their daily lives." The helpers included staff of the local Office of Economic Opportunity center, juvenile court workers, welfare caseworkers, and school personnel. Data were collected by means of informal interviews with the mother, children, and helpers and by participant observation. The author participated by becoming involved in helping to resolve one of the family's problems. The evidence presented for the author's conclusions is primarily in the form of quotations from conversations with the participants.

The author is able to show how each person took for granted certain background features of the situation and assumed that others shared those assumptions. However the actors' background assumptions differed considerably. For example, the mother (who did not speak English) assumed that everyone would know that she could not attend the court hearing because she had to work, while the helpers expected her to attend.

The author describes how each helper saw and was concerned with only one aspect of the family's problems. Further, actions of the helpers appeared to exacerbate the family's difficulties.

Grounded Theory

The grounded theory approach, developed by sociologists Barney G. Glaser and Anselm L. Strauss is concerned exclusively with the generation rather than the testing of theory.[2] Glaser and Strauss are highly critical of what they consider a tendency in sociology to develop grand theory, theory constructed deductively from *a priori* assumptions. When deductive theory is valued, the role of research is to test it. Instead, the grounded theory approach uses research to systematically develop theory. Glaser and Strauss observe that theory based on data can usually not be completely refuted by more data or replaced by another theory,[3] a comment with which many traditional methodologists would strongly disagree.

As with ethnomethodological approaches, a researcher using the grounded theory approach begins with direct observation of social phenomena and unstructured interviewing. The observations are documented in extensive field notes.

A distinction is made between substantive and formal theory. A *substantive* theory is a description and abstraction of what goes on in a particular kind of social setting, for example, hospital wards with dying patients. Analytic abstractions are used in discussing such settings, but no claim is made that the abstractions apply to other situations. In *formal* theory, abstractions and hypotheses about the relationships among these abstractions are developed. These hypotheses should then explain phenomena in many kinds of settings. Formal theory is concerned with a conceptual area of study such as deviant behavior or organizational theory. Ideally, one should begin by developing substantive theory in a particular area and then broaden out to formal theory by using several substantive theories.

Critical concepts in the grounded theory approach include categories (or conceptual categories), properties of categories, the constant comparative method and theoretical sampling.

A *category* is essentially a concept, as that term has been defined earlier in this book, that is, a set of objects or events or a variable. An example used by Glaser and Strauss is the category of the social loss of a dying patient. Glaser and Strauss observed that nurses on wards with terminally ill patients assessed the extent to which the death of a patient would be experienced as a loss by family, friends, or society. Glaser and Strauss found that this assessment helped the nurses to reach an understanding of the death and to know how to behave toward the dying patient.

Properties of categories are aspects or elements of them. They may be things that define the category, ways it is exhibited, conditions for its occurrence and consequences of it. A property of the category of social loss is that patient care tends to vary with nurses' perceptions of social loss.

Theoretical sampling has to do with the selection of persons, groups, or situations to study. In traditional methods random sampling is valued, while in the grounded theory approach the persons or situations to be studied are carefully selected. Since grounded theory unfolds as the researcher goes along, the next person or situation to be studied is chosen so as to best contribute to the further development of the theory. At any one time the researcher is interested in exploring a number of categories, that is, in trying to determine their properties. The next person or situation to be sampled should be one that will be likely to lead to discovery of new properties of important concepts. Of course, in studying that person or situation, one must be open to discovery of insights on other topics as well.

Early in research one tries to minimize differences among the persons or situations one studies, so that one can be confident of the soundness of the basic categories and their properties. Later, differences in sampling units are maximized in order to begin to establish generality of theoretical principles.

Eventually the researcher finds that the category is *theoretically saturated*. This happens when additional instances of the category do not give us additional information, that is, no new properties are being discovered. When saturation occurs one goes on to sample for other categories. The judgment that saturation has occurred should not be made until a wide range of instances have been examined.

Incidents that occur during one's observations are carefully coded as to the categories and properties that they exhibit. A particular incident may be coded in more than one category. Coding merges with the analysis of data through the *constant comparison* method. As one codes, one constantly compares incidents with previous incidents coded in the same category. It is out of this comparison that the properties of categories emerge and their validity is confirmed. The process also leads to the development of new categories.

Coding and analysis begin at the same time that data collection (observation) begins and are on-going. Categories and properties are allowed to emerge from the observational data. In this sense the resulting theory is thought to be grounded on the data.

The grounded theory approach could be used to increase understanding of how social welfare organizations work and of how staff members and clients define their roles and manage their relationships with each other. The researcher would engage in direct observation of the activities in the organization and conduct extensive unstructured interviews with staff and clients. Categories that have impact on the activities of participants would be sought. For example, it might be found that staff defined certain clients as troublemakers. Such a category would be probed for its properties, that is, its definition and its consequences, including what happened to clients defined as troublesome. A theory might be developed for the agency which could contribute to a formal theory of welfare organization functioning or societal response to deviance.

Qualitative Evaluation

Qualitative evaluation makes use of the ideas outlined above to evaluate social programs. In most instances the emphasis is on producing information useful for the further development of programs. As such it is usually more formative than summative. That is, qualitative evaluations usually do not produce conclusions about whether the program was successful or unsuccessful. Rather, detailed descriptions are produced of how participants experience the program and its operation. From these descriptions those concerned can make judgments about whether or not to continue the program or how it should be altered. Sometimes the results of the evaluation are fed back to program staff as the process progresses, rather than waiting until all the data are in.

As indicated above, the usual objectives of a qualitative evaluation are:

1. The production of as complete a description as possible of the components of the program, particularly the interactions among program participants, both staff and clients.
2. A thorough description of the context of the program. What forces external to the program affect its development and course? What do participants bring to the program in the way of beliefs, skills, and knowledge? What social and political factors influence the program?
3. An understanding of how staff and clients experience the program. The researcher attempts to capture how it feels to be a worker or client in the program and to describe what kinds of changes they go through during its course.

As in other forms of qualitative research, the investigator tries to begin work with as few preconceptions as possible about the nature of the program and what he will find. Actual operations rather than plans should be described. Some researchers intentionally begin such evaluations with as little knowledge about the program as possible; they do not even want program officials to tell them its goals. Thus they enter the evaluation situation with only general notions about it.

An important assumption in qualitative evaluation is that programs are dynamic, that is, they change and evolve. Programs are never implemented exactly as planned and they tend to adapt to changing circumstances as they go along. A careful description of these changes and the forces responsible for them is an important part of a qualitative evaluation.

The data for qualitative evaluations are usually obtained through participant observation and informal interviews. The extent to which the researcher is a participant rather than an observer varies. It could be argued that to understand fully how clients experience the program the researcher should become a client. In some rare circumstances that may be possible. On the other hand it would be a rare researcher who would be willing to have himself admitted to a total institution such as a mental hospital or a prison.[4] More commonly the investigator tries to get to know a number of clients, gradually building rapport until intimate conversations can be held in which the clients' real point of view is revealed.

Once the data are in they must be interpreted through the procedures outlined above. Many qualitative researchers believe that the investigator should be personally and intimately involved in such interpretation through his own reflections and introspections on the data. Understanding how other people feel requires an empathic stance on the part of the researcher. The qualitative investigator believes that truth does not lie in mere statistical summaries.

An example of qualitative research on the workings of a social program is a study by Emerson and Pollner of psychiatric emergency teams (PETs)[5] in a regional community mental health clinic. These teams were available to respond to psychiatric emergencies by making field trips to the site of the trouble. A case usually began with a phone call. Often the call came from a relative or other person who was concerned about the disturbed individual. The PET team did not respond to all phone calls reporting emergencies; thus the study focused on its method of selection. Data was gathered by observation of the PET team at work in the office and in the field.

The researchers discovered two general categories of considerations used by the teams in selecting cases. The first provided an ordering of the cases in terms of seriousness and urgency. These considerations included the legal mandate to be concerned with cases in which there was a danger to self, danger to others or grave disability. However, few calls to the clinic were made in the midst of an acute and dangerous crisis, so other considerations were also used in evaluating severity. These included previous knowledge of the case and of similar cases. The team also often transformed the caller's descriptions of the situation by viewing them as overreactions, manipulations, or evidence that the caller was more disturbed than the supposed patient.

Selection of cases did not depend entirely on assessments of severity or urgency. A second category of considerations involved organizational or personal needs. These included bureaucratic or political pressures, geographical location, and assessments of which cases were easiest or most straightforward.

Although not presented as an evaluation per se, this study revealed a great deal about how this particular service works. As such, the information is useful for planning alterations in the management of the program.

Qualitative and Quantitative Approaches

Much recent writing about qualitative and quantitative approaches makes the assumption that they are opposing methods. The quantitative researcher is tempted to reject qualitative methodology on the grounds that it is unscientific. While all research is affected by the bias of the investigator (for example, all studies involve a selection of what is to be observed) the biases are more likely to be public in quantitative approaches and thus are subject to the scrutiny of others. In this sense, the quantitative researcher views qualitative findings as hopelessly contaminated by unrevealed biases. Further, without measurements that can be manipulated statistically or mathematically we cannot be precise in our descriptions and often cannot specify causal relationships.

On the other hand, qualitative enthusiasts reject quantitative methods as too narrow and restrictive for the investigation of important questions. Were we to use only quantitative methods we would miss understanding important parts of the world; for example, we would not have a real understanding of people's thoughts and feelings.

In my view, the two approaches should not be viewed as being oppositional. Properly used, both can enhance our understanding of the world. Much of the sense of opposition comes from the underlying conflict of the philosophical positions of logical positivism and phenomenology. But these positions can and should be separated from the respective research methods. The philosophical debates are fascinating intellectually, but they are not critical to the methods used by scientists. The methods themselves need not be in conflict. In fact, in some studies they can be used in conjunction with each other in a complementary way.[6]

Campbell has observed that researchers using qualitative methods inevitably move toward making comparisons among persons in different situations.[7] (Comparison appears to be a fundamental process in science.) This, he argues, is the essence of an experiment; the comparison of contrasting groups. He suggests that it will be found desirable to increase the rigor of the comparisons. Hence qualitative methods will eventually take on the essential elements of quantitative inquiry.

Qualitative methods may often lead to important understandings missed in quantitative research. All research in the social sciences (and perhaps other sciences as well) begins with qualitative understandings, a sense of the situation or the problem that as yet cannot be expressed precisely or quantitatively. Sometimes it is useful to develop these understandings further before engaging in quantitative studies. In evaluative studies it may be useful to engage in both kinds of investigation, determining the balance between them by the objectives of the study.

Often the debate about the acceptability of qualitative data misses the point. Although for some purposes (such as statistical and mathematical manipulation) it is desirable that measures yield numerical values, the critical issue is not whether data can be expressed in numbers, but the soundness of the data. One criterion for soundness is that of replicability. It is important to make observations in such a way that others could see the same things we do if the process were repeated. The effort to make observations replicable has characterized quantitative methods, even though many important studies have not been repeated. As qualitative methods develop more rigorous approaches to observation, it should be possible (at least in theory) to make their data replicable also.

Notes

1. Reyes Ramos, A Case in Point: An Ethnomethodological Study of a Poor Mexican American Family, *Social Science Quarterly*, 53(4):905-919, 1973.
2. Barney G. Glaser and Anselm L. Strauss, *The Discovery of Grounded Theory*, Chicago: Aldine Publishing, 1967.
3. *Ibid*, p. 4.
4. On Being Sane in Insane Places, *Science*, 179:250-258, 1973.
5. Robert M. Emerson and Melvin Pollner, Policies and Practices of Psychiatric Case Selection, *Sociology of Work and Occupations*, 5(1):75-96, 1978.
6. Charles S. Reichart and Thomas D. Cook, Beyond Qualitative *ver-*

sus Quantitative Methods, in Cook and Reichart, Eds., *Qualitative and Quantitative Methods in Evaluation Research*, Beverly Hills, Ca.: Sage Publications, 1979.

7. Donald T. Campbell, Degrees of Freedom and the Case Study, in Cook and Reichart.

Bibliography

Books about how to do qualitative research include:

Howard S. Becker, *Sociological Work*, Chicago: Aldine, 1970.

Robert Bogdan and Steven J. Taylor, *Introduction to Qualitative Research Methods*, New York: Wiley, 1975.

Thomas D. Cook and Charles S. Reichart, *Qualitative and Quantitative Methods in Evaluation Research*, Beverly Hills, Ca.: Sage, 1979.

Norman K. Denzin, *The Research Act*, New York: McGraw Hill, 1978.

W. Filsted, *Qualitative Methodology*, Chicago: Markham, 1970.

Barney G. Glaser and Anselm L. Strauss, *The Discovery of Grounded Theory*, Chicago: Aldine, 1967.

Michael Q. Patton, *Qualitative Evaluation Methods*, Beverly Hills, Ca.: Sage, 1980.

Some qualitative research studies are:

Erving Goffman, *Asylums: Essays on the Social Situation of Mental Patients and Other Inmates*, New York: Anchor, 1961.

Dwight Frankfather, *The Aged in the Community*, New York: Praeger, 1977.

Gerald D. Suttles, *The Social Order of the Slum*, Chicago: University of Chicago Press, 1968.

8

Ethics in Research

Values are central to the work of human service professionals. They provide the rationale and context of our work. They specify the limits of proper professional behavior and serve as a guide for difficult decisions. Frequently professionals encounter situations in which values are in conflict. Should you assist a mother to abort a deformed fetus? Should parental rights or the child's interests govern? Should you report a welfare recipient whose grant is too large?

Research occasionally has some real or potentially damaging effect on the persons who participate. The effect may range from minor inconvenience to denial of effective treatment to actual psychological damage to the individual. But the research may have important benefits to other people. Hence the conflict of values: the rights of subjects of the research as opposed to the need to conduct studies to find ways of helping people in the future. Complicating matters is the fact that the potential personal harm is immediate, while the potential broader benefits will come later.

In recent years there has been an increase in concern about

ethical issues in social and medical research. In part this concern
is due to several studies which clearly have been unethical. In
this century, the most notorious were the programs of medical
study in Nazi Germany, studies conducted without regard for human life. Concern about these experiments led to the Nuremberg
code (1947), a set of ethical principles which still guides medical
researchers.

Unfortunately, this country has not been free of unethical
medical and social experiments. An example is a study by the
United States Public Health Service conducted from the early
1930s to the early 1970s. The study involved 400 black men in
Macon County, Alabama who had syphilis. Throughout the period of the study the men went untreated for the disease, often
passing it on to mates and fathering children with congenital syphilis.[1] Another example is from social psychology. In an investigation of the nature of social influence on people, subjects were
pressured into giving what they thought were painful and harmful
electric shocks to other subjects. The shocks were imaginary and
the other subjects were accomplices of the investigator.[2] It is
likely that the procedures resulted in considerable conflict in
some subjects, particularly after they learned they were duped.

Social concern over studies such as these has led to extensive
legal regulation of research. The first such laws established regulations on the handling of human subjects in federally financed
research. Now many states have laws dealing with research concerning human subjects and universities and other institutions
have established procedures for such research. Today, mechanisms for the protection of human subjects revolve around the
institutional review board (IRB), a group established by an institution to review all research which might involve harm to individuals. IRBs are required to determine whether subjects are adequately protected and whether the benefits of the research
outweigh the risks.

As in all areas of human conduct, the first line of defense
against unethical research is the moral character of the researcher. Unfortunately, as history painfully demonstrates, a few
researchers can be unethical. Besides that, an essentially moral
scientist may be blinded by his zeal or have too inflated a view of
the likely benefits of his research.

Confidentiality

The danger of release of sensitive information about individuals is perhaps the most common risk in social research. The right to privacy is very important in our culture. We want to be able to control the information that other people have about us. Hence confidentiality is an important ethical principle in the helping professions and in social research. Often in social research we collect data about people or about their opinions and ideas that they would not like others to know. As part of the research process researchers guarantee confidentiality to participants and take steps to make sure that guarantee holds.

Most of the threats to confidentiality are seemingly trivial, but are important to think about in the administration of research. Research staff may be careless in handling documents containing sensitive information, leaving them lying around where unauthorized persons might be able to look at them. In addition, project staff sometimes gossip about subjects of research, much in the same way that workers in social agencies sometimes improperly gossip about their cases.

Several steps can be taken to minimize threats to confidentiality. Staff should be impressed with the necessity to maintain confidentiality and access to sensitive materials should be limited to as few persons as possible. Documents containing personal information should be kept in locked cabinets when they are not in use. In some studies it may not be necessary to record the participant's name or other identifying information. However, other studies require linking information obtained at several different points or from several sources. In such studies the linking may be done by means of case numbers rather than through names. It is a good idea to strip names from data collection instruments, by, for example, tearing off the page with the name on it. A cross listing of names and case numbers can be kept in a separate place, accessible only to one person. Identifying data should be destroyed as soon as they are no longer needed. Finally, of course, reports of the research should never contain descriptions of individuals that are identifiable.

Sometimes there are more serious threats to confidentiality. Some researchers have faced subpoenas from courts or legislative committees for information about subjects. Such legal actions cause great difficulties for researchers. Some researchers who investigate matters that might be subject to subpoena have even gone so far as to store identifying data in Swiss bank vaults, presumably out of the reach of legal procedure, although it is not clear that taking such action would be successful in assuring confidentiality.

Physicians, lawyers, and clerics enjoy privilege; that is, communications with them are protected by law from legal process. In some states social workers also have privilege. However, communications with researchers are not protected.

Another issue in confidentiality arises when the opinions and activities of public officials are studied. Suppose the researcher learns information that the official considers confidential but which if revealed might promote the public good or prevent a public harm. Undoubtedly officials cannot expect to enjoy the right to privacy to the same extent as others. But how much privacy they can expect is a matter of some debate in discussions of research ethics.

Other Risks

Generally social research does not involve threats to life or health as in some medical research, but there can be some potential harm beyond revealing sensitive information. Often the risks are relatively minor, perhaps some discomfort created by research procedures or the inconvenience of having to spend time on research tasks. At other times the research plan may call for procedures that could cause conflict, either within the individual or with others. Often researchers ask questions about things the individual has tried to forget, and as a result disturbing feelings are reawakened. The researcher must do everything possible to limit these potential harms. All sensitive questions must be fully justified by the research objectives. Questions should not be asked out of mere curiosity.

Experimental Studies

Evaluation studies involving experimental designs often require that participants in the study be denied services or receive services that may be less effective. Much debate has been generated by this requirement, some people asserting that it is essential for sound conclusions about effectiveness and that the ethical issues raised can be overcome. Others assert that it is plainly unethical to deny services to anyone, especially if the criteria for denial is a random process (rather than giving service to those most in need or most likely to benefit).

Those who defend experimental evaluation argue that it is not unethical to deny a service that has not yet proven effective. Further, there are often not enough resources to provide a newly developed service to everyone, so a random process may in fact be the most ethical way to select those to receive it. In other situations, if the problem is not an immediate crisis, the ethical difficulties can be reduced by arranging for the control group to receive treatment at a later date. Thus treatment is delayed rather than denied. In still other cases an alternative treatment can be provided rather than having an untreated control group.

Informed Consent

The idea of *informed consent* is central to the protection of human subjects. Most writers on research ethics hold that whenever subjects are at risk, they should be informed of the risks and given the opportunity to decide whether or not to participate in the research. Current governmental regulations[3] require that the subject be given:

1. An explanation of the purposes of the research, a description of what will happen, and an indication of how long his participation will be expected.
2. A description of "any reasonably foreseeable risks or discomforts."
3. A description of any benefits expected from the research, either to him or others.
4. "Disclosure of appropriate alternative procedures or courses of treatment...."
5. A discussion of confidentiality of records identifying the subject.

Other information may be required under certain circumstances. This must be given to the subject in language that he can understand. After the information is provided the subject should be given the opportunity to decide whether or not to participate.

No coercion may be used to secure his cooperation. If he refuses to participate he must not be denied services or otherwise punished. The subject must be permitted to discontinue participation at any time. In most cases all of the above should be written out and signed by the subject to indicate his consent. However, merely obtaining a signature on a form does not constitute informed consent. The researcher (or his representative) must not simply hand the subject a form to be signed but should explain the conditions and procedures carefully and be ready to answer questions.

In some circumstances obtaining truly informed consent is problematic. Persons who are experiencing psychological or physical pain or who are otherwise in stress may feel they should consent because of the situation, perhaps in order to receive service. Prisoners and other institutionalized persons often are vulnerable to subtle or even blatant coercion. Finally, children and persons' with diminished capacity (the mentally ill or mentally incapacitated) present special difficulties of consent. In such research, informed consent should be obtained both from the subject (where possible) and from someone who is able to represent his interests, such as a parent, other relative, or legal representative.

According to governmental regulations, in social science research that involves very little risk to the subject it is not necessary to obtain formal informed consent. An example is a survey in which there is no danger of breach of confidentiality and which does not contain potentially troubling questions. In situations in which it is assumed that persons are able to refuse answers to certain questions, consent is implied by the subject's agreement to participate overall. It usually is unnecessary to obtain informed consent when existing records are used in the research and there is no way to identify subjects from them. Still another example involves observation of behavior in public places, for example in crowds, where individuals cannot be identified and people cannot reasonably expect their behavior to be private. Similarly, research on the professional actions of public officials does not require their informed consent.

DECEPTION

In the past some social science research has involved deception of subjects, as in the example given earlier in the chapter. It is difficult, if not impossible, to study behavior in certain contexts if the subjects are told the purpose of the research. For example, suppose the research concerns the extent to which people are influenced by other people. If we tell subjects we want to know how much their ideas and behavior are affected by others, the responses we get will probably be different than if they are not informed about our purposes.

Current attitudes and regulations make it very difficult to conduct research involving deception, unless the deception is very mild and benign. The ethics of research involving deception remains a murky issue. If any deception is used it is essential to debrief subjects after the procedures are completed, to explain what went on and to reassure them that their own behavior was not bad.

CULTURAL CONSIDERATIONS

The researcher who conducts studies involving persons with ethnic, cultural, and social class backgrounds different from his own must be aware that such differences may have ethical implications. In particular, sensitive information is culturally defined. For example, discussions of sexuality may not be considered sensitive by some whereas others may consider it a forbidden topic.

FEDERAL REGULATIONS AND INSTITUTIONAL REVIEW
BOARDS

Federal regulations were originally developed in the context of medical research and were subsequently applied to social research. Unfortunately, the concepts and rules that fit the investigation of drugs and other medical procedures do not always apply to the social sciences. Recently, federal regulations have been altered to take into account the special circumstances of social research. Federal regulations no longer require review by institutional review boards of federally funded research involving surveys or interviews, observation of public behavior, the study of existing documents, and research on educational techniques, except when subjects can be identified and release of information could be damaging. Such freedom from regulation obviously does not release the researcher from ethical responsibilities.

Other Ethical Considerations

Thus far this chapter has been concerned entirely with problems of protection of human subjects from the risks of research. But other ethical principles apply as well. Most scientists adhere to the principle that research findings should be reported honestly and completely. Data should not be manipulated to support one's own preconceptions and findings should not be held back because they are damaging to one's theses.

This principle, however, may conflict with other ethical prescriptions in certain circumstances. Sometimes research is carried out with a primarily social action purpose, rather than to obtain objective data about the world. At other times, a researcher may have data which could be used to the detriment of beneficiaries of social programs. No hard and fast rules can be given for resolving such ethical dilemmas. They must be dealt with on a case by case basis.

Summary

Research in the human services often encounters troubling ethical issues. These include confidentiality, the necessity of informed consent, and the assessment of risks to subjects. In addition, some studies may involve problems of consent of persons of diminished capacity and the ethics of deception. Experimental evaluations must deal with the ethics of denying potentially beneficial services to some people.

Besides the obligation to protect the interests of subjects, scientists have other ethical responsibilities as well. These include the obligation to report findings honestly and completely.

Notes

1. James H. Jones, *Bad Blood: The Scandalous Story of the Tuskegee Experiment—When Government Doctors Played God and Science Went Mad*, New York: Free Press, 1981.
2. S. Milgram, Behavioral Study of Obedience, *Journal of Abnormal and Social Psychology*, 67:371-78, 1963.

3. 45 CFR part 46, Federal Register *46*(16):8366-8392, 1981.
4. *Ibid*.

Bibliography

Some of the many works on ethics in human service research are:

American Psychological Association, *Ethical Principles in the Conduct of Research with Human Participants*, Washington, D. C.: 1973.

Edward Diener and Rick Crandell, *Ethics in Social and Behavioral Research*, Chicago: University of Chicago Press, 1978.

N. Hersey and R. D. Miller, *Human Experimentation and the Law*, Germantown, Md.: Aspen Systems Corp., 1976.

J. Katz, *Experimentation with Human Beings*, New York: Russell Sage Foundation, 1972.

H. C. Kelman, *A Time to Speak: On Human Values and Social Research*, San Francisco: Jossey-Bass, 1968.

E. C. Kennedy, *Human Rights and Psychological Research*, New York: Crowell, 1975.

PART III

The Details of Research Methodology

9

Design and Causality

In this chapter we discuss in greater detail issues concerning the design of various studies. Since design is very much concerned with the conditions for making assertions about causal connections, the chapter ends with a discussion of the nature of causality.

The design of a research project is the plan for carrying it out. It provides the details of the process necessary to answer the questions posed by a study. The design should grow out of the specification of the problem, taking into account the limitations the researcher faces. In most applied situations the design is very much affected by the limitations of money, personnel, and time. As a result, designing a research project is a matter of trade-offs among competing considerations. Certain important principles should govern these trade-offs.

The design of a study has several components which can be expressed by the following questions:

1. What is to be the unit of analysis for our study? Will our research questions be answered best by focusing on individuals, families, communities, states, or some other social entity?
2. Once we have chosen our unit of analysis how should we se-

lect the particular subjects to be studied (our sample)? We
must also decide whether to study groups with different experiences. For example, if we are evaluating a program we
might decide to compare a group that went through the program with a group that did not.
3. What information should we get about the people (or other
   units of analysis) that we decide to study? That is, what variables should we have in our study?
4. How should we get the information about the variables (collect
   the data)? Should we use self-administered questionnaires, interviews, or observations?
5. What should be the structure of our data collection? What
   should be the timing in relation to other things our subjects
   may be experiencing such as treatment? Do we need to collect
   information only once or at several points, for example, before, during, and after participation in a social program?
6. Once we have the data, how are they to be analyzed and
   interpreted?

Obviously design depends on the kind of study. We recall the
distinction made earlier between descriptive studies and those
that attempt to reveal causal relationships. In descriptive studies
the primary design problems have to do with sampling and data
collection (particularly questionnaire construction). The design of
these is discussed in Chapters 5 and 6.

The design of studies of causal relationships involves a special
set of problems which we will address in the remainder of this
chapter. Most studies in the social sciences and human services
are at least implicitly concerned with causal relationships. In
many it is asserted that the purpose is only to try to find out if
certain variables are associated. But knowing that variables are
associated does not do much good unless we also suspect that
they are causally linked. Even studies that start out as purely
descriptive or exploratory efforts may turn to discussions of possible causal relationships.

In the social sciences, finding the causes of things is usually
expressed in terms of determining what causes the fluctuation or
change in a variable. Sometimes the variable we want to explain
(the effect or dependent variable) is the occurrence or nonoccurrence of an event, for example, whether somebody gets a job or is

hospitalized. In such cases the variable can be thought of as having two values. Other times, it has more than two, as might be the case with a measure of social functioning.

The causes are also variables (called independent variables). Causes may be events, in which case the variable again has two values, occurrence or nonoccurrence, for example, whether or not someone has been in counseling. Causes may also be variables with more than two values. An example of a causal variable which might have more than two values is motivation for improvement.

To determine the existence of a causal relationship between two variables we must set up a contrast. To measure the effects of a counseling program we must study persons who went through the program and those who did not, or at least look at persons who received it in varying amounts. Similarly, the outcomes must also vary. If everyone does superbly, whether or not they went through the program, we will not be able to detect causal relationships.

In some studies we start out with an hypothesis about the causal connection between a single independent and a single dependent variable. More often, however, we are concerned with many dependent and/or many independent variables. For example:

1. We may think that a given effect has many causes; for example, improvement while in counseling may be the result of many things. If this is the case, we want to have variables in our study representing each possibility. We would then try to determine which of the variables are most important (major causal factors) and which are less so.
2. Conversely, we might be interested in looking at only one or two independent variables and several possible effects. For example, in a study of the outcomes of counseling we might look at changes in self esteem, family relationships, and functioning on the job.
3. We may wish to examine only one cause or effect but devise several ways of measuring it. For example, we might engage in a study of the causes of depression in which changes in eating, sleeping, and communication habits are measured.

Although most studies involve more than one independent and/or more than one dependent variable, for the purposes of the discussion that follows we will focus primarily on the connection between a single independent and a single dependent variable.

The first step in determining whether a causal relationship is present is to find out whether the variables are associated. For example, we must find out whether or not people who went through the counseling program did better than those who didn't. If we think that motivation causes variation in social functioning we must find out if there is an association between the two. An association means that higher motivation goes with higher levels of functioning while lower motivation goes with lower levels of functioning, or vice versa. Usually (but not always) if there is a causal relationship an association is found. Unfortunately, the converse is not necessarily true; that is, the existence of an association does not demonstrate a causal connection. For example, we might discover that persons who went through the counseling program did better than those who did not, but this does not mean that the improvement is the result of counseling.

If we have an association between two variables that we think might indicate a causal relationship, several things must be taken into account before we can be confident of this conclusion. To begin with the causal connection must be sensible. Things can be statistically related to each other without any reasonable causal connection.

We will assume we are studying two variables and that it is reasonable to think they might be causally connected. Even if we have an association, however, and it is reasonable to think that our independent variable might be causing the dependent variable, there are usually a number of alternative explanations for the association other than the causal one we are thinking of. First of all, it is possible that we have gotten the direction of causality wrong: perhaps our dependent variable is causing our independent variable rather than the other way around.

The best way to deal with the direction of causality problem is to pay very close attention to the order of events. In a cause and effect relationship the cause must come before the effect. So we try to find out which event occurred first.

It is also possible that the relationship between the two variables is reciprocal, that is, they cause changes in each other. Perhaps improvement causes an individual to go into counseling which in turn inspires more improvement. Again this possible relationship is dealt with by trying to establish carefully the order of events.

Finally, it is possible that some other variable may have been responsible for the association we observe. For example, the people who choose to undergo counseling may be more motivated to improve than those who did not and therefore might have improved anyway. The situation might be diagrammed as in Figure 9.1. The dotted line indicates an observed association that is not a causal connection, while the solid lines indicate verified causal connections.

In most social research there are many alternative explanations possible for the observed association between independent and dependent variables. These are referred to as threats to the validity of the conclusions and as extraneous or intervening variables. In the design of studies of causal relationships much effort is put into trying to deal with alternative explanations, usually by making them less likely. That is, we try to design studies in such a way as to make it unlikely that other variables could explain the causal relationships we want to claim exist. We call this the *control* of alternative explanations.

There are two ways of achieving control over alternative explanations:

1. We can actively manipulate the independent variable (the thing we think of as a cause) in what is called an experimental design (discussed at greater length in Chapter 4). This may mean establishing a treatment and a nontreatment group, or several groups comprised of people receiving various levels of treatment. Paradoxically, although we control the designation of the groups it is important that the assignment of people to them be determined randomly.
2. We may attempt to achieve control passively through the statistical analysis of data. To do so, we must have data on variables that represent alternative explanations. For example, if

FIGURE 9.1

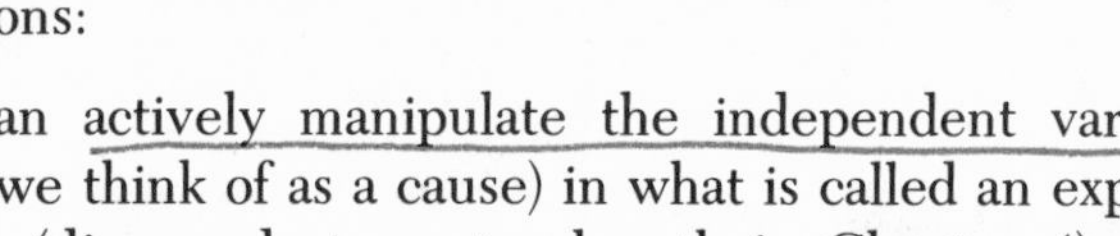

Motivation _verified causal_

→Improvement

Counseling — _not causal_

we think motivation is an alternative explanation for the link between counseling and improvement, we must have data on this factor. We could then look at the relationship between counseling and improvement within each level of motivation. If it disappeared in this analysis we would be led to conclude that motivation is a reasonable explanation for the link between counseling and improvement. On the other hand, if the relationship held up at each level of motivation, then motivation is unlikely to be an alternative explanation.

This approach to control requires that we try before-hand to think of as many alternative explanations as possible so we will be able to collect data on them. In contrast, a well-constructed experimental study need not anticipate all possible alternative explanations.

Statistical control is never as satisfying as experimental control. It usually is not possible to reject alternative explanations entirely through statistical control. However, there are many situations in which we want to study cause-effect relationships but we are unable to use experiments for practical or ethical reasons. In such cases we will go ahead and do research, depending on statistical manipulations to get at causes.

Experimental Designs

In experimental designs we actively manipulate the variable we think is a cause. This allows us to eliminate a number of alternative explanations. A third variable cannot have been responsible for differences in the independent variable, nor is it possible that the causal direction is reversed or the relationship reciprocal.

For example, if we decide who should receive counseling, then variations in client motivation can't enter into the decision to receive counseling. In actual practice we make the decisions randomly; that way we know even the researcher cannot be the source of an alternative explanation. If the receipt of counseling is purely a matter of chance, then nothing else can have caused its variation.

Of course, the above is somewhat idealized. In actual practice it is possible for an experiment that is rigorously designed to be affected by third variables if people drop out of the study. Persons with low motivation might tend to drop out of the experimental group so that at the end of the study the groups are no longer random.

QUASI-EXPERIMENTAL DESIGNS

In recent years there has been a great deal written about quasi-experimental designs. These are designs for the evaluation of programs in which random assignment is not used and causal connections are explored statistically. When quasi-experimental designs are used it is important to pay attention to alternative explanations. We do so by trying to anticipate and classify them beforehand.

The concept of threats to validity was most thoroughly developed by Campbell and Stanley.[1] Recently, Cook and Campbell have revised and extended the classification of threats to validity first presented by Campbell and Stanley.[2] The discussion here draws heavily on the formulation of Cook and Campbell.

Cook and Campbell distinguish four types of validity: (1) statistical conclusion validity, (2) internal validity, (3) construct validity, and (4) external validity. Threats to validity are considered within each of these categories. The present discussion leaves out construct validity, as that has been discussed in the context of measurement validity in Chapter 2.

In our discussion of these categories we will use the example of a counseling program evaluation in which one group received service and another did not.

Random or chance factors.   Suppose we found that those receiving service did better than the other group. There is an association between receipt of service and improvement. However, it is possible the difference is due to random, nonsystematic influences. This threat exists even in randomized experiments; that is, even when groups are formed randomly it is possible they will be different before treatment.

Statistical analysis is used to deal with these random, nonsystematic influences. Although is never possible to rule out this threat completely, the probability that it has occurred can be determined, through the process of statistical hypothesis testing described in Chapter 12. If the probability of random factors is very low, the association we observe is said to be *significant* and is thought of as a real association. A significant association still does not mean we have a causal relationship, so if we find significance we must go on to consider other threats to validity.

All statistical tests are based on certain assumptions about the data. That is, certain things have to be true for the conclusions to be accurate. If those things are not true the statistical conclusions may be invalid. Beyond the problem of the violation of assumptions, the situation in which we do not find a statistically significant relationship is particularly problematic. If this happened in our example, we could not claim that persons in counseling do better than those not in counseling. Paradoxically, we also cannot claim that persons in counseling fare the same or worse. (Statisticians would say that we cannot prove the null hypothesis; this expression is explained in Chapter 12.)

An observed association may be nonsignificant even when there is a causal relationship between the two variables. This distressing state of affairs can occur because the statistical test for significance may not be powerful enough to detect the association. The power of a test is the probability that it will detect a real difference. Two reasons that power might be low are:

1. Sample size. If sample size is too small an association may be difficult to detect.
2. Too much extraneous or error variation in the variables. A lot of extraneous variation in outcome within our groups would make it difficult to detect differences between them. The within-groups variation is sometimes called *error variation* and refers both to errors of measurement and to other sources of random variation.

If the problem is caused by errors of measurement the solution, of course, is to use more reliable measures. If the within-group variation is due to other factors, other solutions must be sought. Sometimes we reduce within-group variation by selecting cases that are relatively homogeneous, cases that would have similar outcomes if they were not exposed to treatment. This solution may cause problems with external validity or generalizability. That is, if we limit our study group we may not be able to generalize our findings very much. Finally it is possible sometimes to reduce within-group variation by removing it statistically.

Sometimes within-group variation is increased by faulty implementation of treatment or variations in the amount of treatment received by various persons. It is thus desirable to have control over the provision of treatment, to assure that all members of the treatment group receive the same amount.

It is possible to estimate the power of an experiment before the study is undertaken. Through statistical calculations we can estimate the probability of obtaining significant results if our hypothesis is correct. Unfortunately such power analyses are rarely done.

Internal Validity. We now assume that our statistical tests showed significant results: our counseling group did significantly better than our nontreatment group. This brings us to another set of alternative explanations called threats to internal validity. *Internal validity* has to do with whether or not we can infer that a statistically significant association indicates a causal connection within our particular study group. Threats to internal validity include:

1. *History*. By history we mean events that happen during the study, other than the experimental intervention. It is possible that our treatment group had experiences the control group did not have which led to their improvement. For example, suppose we instituted a new form of income maintenance in one state and compared that state to another where the usual programs continue. If economic conditions improved in the experimental state and did not improve in the control state, differences in outcome may be due to the altered economy rather than the experimental intervention.

2. *Maturation*. Changes during the study which are not due to treatment or external events may arise from a person's natural growth and change over time. It is possible that people in the experimental group will change more or less than those in the control group. For example, people in our counseling group might just grow out of their problems while those not receiving counseling do not.

3. *Selection*. The two groups may be different to begin with. Un-

less we have random assignment, the treatment group may do
better than the control even without treatment. The idea of
selection overlaps with the ideas of history and maturation.
Sometimes additional threats to validity are identified as interactions of selection with other things like maturation or history. This simply means that cases were selected into experimental and control groups that had different histories (sets of
experiences) or rates of maturation.

4. *Mortality.* In nearly every social study some persons are lost
from the initial samples. People in either group may refuse to
complete the study or be unable to do so (a move, an illness,
and so forth). It is possible that more people will drop out of
one group than the other. More importantly, the departures
from one group may be different from those of the other. The
differences in the samples at the end of the study may then be
due to this factor. Even in experimental studies in which random assignment is used, differential mortality can make the
groups too imbalenced for comparison at the end.

5. *Statistical regression.* Statistical regression occurs when we select persons for the experimental group because they are extreme cases while the control group is not so extreme. For
example, we might select persons for counseling because they
were very depressed and compare them with persons who
were not so depressed. One might select students for a com-
pensatory education program because they are doing poorly in
school and compare them with a group that is not doing as
badly. Statistical regression is not an easy concept to grasp. A
full explanation of the idea would require statistical reasoning
that is beyond the scope of this book. The problem with selecting extreme cases is that there are almost always random
or nonsystematic factors that contribute to making the cases
extreme at the time we do the selection. Later on when we
test for the effects of treatment, these factors may not be operating. When we measure the cases later, they will have, on
the average, regressed toward a more normal position (this is
called *regression toward the mean*). While this might not happen with any one case, it will tend to happen to the group as
a whole. If the control group cases were less extreme at the
time of selection their regression toward the mean will be less.
Regression effects do not occur if we select extreme cases and
then assign them randomly to experimental and control groups.

In that situation, both groups will regress toward the mean, presumably about the same amount, and comparisons will be valid. Regression effects are often identified with errors of measurement. An unreliable measurement procedure may identify persons as being extreme at one point and not later on. While such errors do contribute to regression effects, they are not the whole story, since random factors other than measurement go into determining an individual's position on a variable at any one time.

6. *Testing and measurement.* There are several ways measurement operations may adversely affect the outcome of the study. First, if a measurement like a test or attitude scale is applied several times, people may remember it and respond similarly each time. If this were the case, the instrument would not be measuring true changes. Second, if a measurement is applied several times it is possible the instrument itself might change. For example, if the measurements involve judgments the judges may become more experienced or more fatigued or may shift their interpretation of evidence. Finally, there may be floor or ceiling effects in the measurement. The measurement procedure may not yield accurate results when the variable has extreme values. For example, a measure of depression might not do a very good job of distinguishing very severe depression from somewhat less severe depression.

7. *Treatment contamination.* This occurs when the control group receives some treatment, even when it is not supposed to.

A formal experiment with randomized assignment of subjects to treatment and control groups or to two different treatments theoretically controls most threats to internal validity. This kind of assignment will randomize the effects of history, maturation, selection, and statistical regression. Usually it also will randomize the effects of testing and measurement, although it is possible to have an interaction of treatment and testing. A before measure might sensitize people to the treatment so that what appears to be a treatment effect is really a combination of testing and treatment.

Random assignment alone cannot control for mortality. It is, however, often possible to take steps to reduce the rate of subject loss from a study. If there are only a few losses from both experimental and control groups it is unlikely that mortality is a significant threat to validity. Also, it is sometimes possible to estimate the effects of mortality on our results through statistical analysis.

Listing the possible threats to validity may help the researcher think about alternative explanations in a proposed study and help readers analyze research reports. Not all of these threats will be important or applicable in any particular research project.

External Validity. Internal validity is concerned with establishing that a causal relationship exists between variables as measured in a particular study. Once causality is established we usually will want to generalize in two respects. First, we want to assert that the variables as measured represent concepts that have a larger meaning. This stage of generalization is called construct validity and is discussed in Chapter 2 and Chapter 11. Second, we will want to claim that the causal relationship holds in groups of people other than those studied. The latter generalization is called external validity.

Problems of external validity primarily revolve around sampling issues. The group actually studied is thought of as representative of a larger population to which we want to generalize. Ideally, the sample should be random (or otherwise probability based). If it is randomly chosen then statistical analysis will tell us how much confidence we can have in claiming that the results hold for the population. The amount of confidence is expressed in terms of probability statements, that is, the probability that a relationship holds in the population.

However, many times in social research our study group is not a random sample from a population. We often study a particular social program and locality with clients that are not randomly chosen. Thus we cannot generalize on the basis of statistical analysis alone. In these cases inferential statistical analysis will rule out the possibility that random factors in the study group are causing the relationship (as discussed above), but this will not provide an adequate basis for generalizing to a population.

Nonetheless, we do want to be able to generalize from nonrandom samples. The extent to which this is legitimate is a matter of some debate. Such generalizations depend on non-statistical reasoning. If a relationship exists in our sample we ask whether we expect it to be present in a larger population and why. We must think about how our sample differs from the larger population and whether the differences seem likely to be important. In the process it is important to try to specify the limits of our generalization, by noting the characteristics of persons to whom the results apply.

For example, suppose we are doing an experiment on a new treatment program with youthful offenders in a particular county. Judges refer clients to this program who are then randomly assigned to the new treatment or to traditional supervision. Suppose the treatment group does better and there are no serious threats to internal validity. We have problems in generalizing on two counts. First, the judge selected a nonrandom group for referral and second, the youthful offenders in this county cannot be expected to be representative of those in the whole country. At most we will be able to generalize to that group similar to those in our study. Thus we will need to describe our study group carefully and even then we cannot be sure we have identified those characteristics important for generalization.

Usually, discussions of the generality of findings also include comparisons of the characteristics of those studied with those of the whole population. The differences can be useful in describing the limitations of the generalizations. Sometimes when a study group is found to be similar to a population in several ways the researcher uses this as evidence for the soundness of his generalizations. This is risky, however, since again we cannot be sure we have identified the right characteristics for comparisons.

The process of examining the generalization of findings from a nonrandom sample obviously involves a great many judgments in which the investigator probably has some stake. Other researchers and practitioners might well reach different conclusions. As a result, claims of generality are often subject to argument and can be settled conclusively only by replication of the study. As noted earlier, one of the principal functions of replication is to test the limits to which findings can be generalized. Studies should be repeated in other locations, using study groups that differ in important ways from those studied earlier and possibly using different measures and procedures.

Types of Quasi-Experimental Designs. We have talked about quasi-experimental designs at several points in this book under various other names. Such designs may be categorized as follows:

1. Nonequivalent comparison group designs. These are designs in which two or more groups are exposed to different treat-

ment conditions (one of which may be a nontreatment control condition) without random assignment. The groups cannot be assumed equivalent before treatment, so statistical analysis must be depended upon for control of alternative explanations.

2. *Interrupted time series designs*. In this design a group is followed over a period of time. At some point a treatment is introduced (the time series is interrupted). Several measures of the dependent variable (ideally, a large number of these) are taken before and after treatment. The series of observations is analyzed to see if there are changes after the treatment. This design is logically equivalent to the AB design discussed in Chapter 3. Sometimes more than one group is followed in which case we may have a combination of nonequivalent comparison group and interrupted time series designs. Such a study is similar to the multiple baseline design of Chapter 3.

3. *Passive observational designs*. In this type of study variations in dependent and independent variables are observed only once (a cross-sectional study) or several times over a short period. It may not be possible to identify clear comparison groups; instead we depend on natural variation in the independent variable and on statistical analysis.

Causality

In this section we discuss, somewhat more theoretically, what is meant by cause, since the detection of causality is a central objective of research.[3]

The idea of causality is one that has occupied philosophers for centuries. We may think that we are being perfectly clear when we say that something causes something else but philosophers have found all kinds of problems in such statements. Practicing scientists have much less difficulty with causal statements; nonetheless, it is useful to have some sense of the problems involved. What follows is an attempt to find a path through difficult terrain, without exploring all of the possible pitfalls. It is a path designed for the social scientist, and thus is concerned with causality in social relations and human behavior. The positions we take would not satisfy most philosophers but are intended to be practical for our purposes.

Some philosophers have argued that the idea of cause exists only in our minds and that there is nothing in the real world that corresponds to it. Since this is the case, the argument continues, notions of causality ought to be eliminated from scientific writing and descriptions sought in its stead. However, it is obvious that the idea of causation is deeply ingrained in us (whether it is biologically or culturally determined doesn't matter here). All of us see causality and certainly we all act as if it exists. Indeed, the idea that we can make this a better world is based on the assumption that our actions can cause change. We will assume it is meaningful to talk about the cause(s) of an event.

Probably the simplest view of causation is this: we can say that event *A* is the cause of effect *B* if *A* preceeds *B* in time and if, whenever *A* occurs, *B* occurs. To this conception of cause other conditions are sometimes added. It may be required that whenever *B* has occurred *A* has to have occurred previously (*A* has to be necessary as well as sufficient for *B*) and sometimes it is required that there be some kind of sensible link between *A* and *B*, some kind of mechanism connecting them.

There are many aspects to the notion of cause; we will discuss each in turn.

Time precedence. Some philosophers have difficulty with the notion of time precedence as an element of causality. Instead they insist that the effect occur simultaneously with the cause. If it appears there is a separate cause and effect, it is only that we are looking at the ends of a chain of causes and effects. Thus we cannot accurately say that *A* causes *B* if they are separate events and instead should try to fill in the intermediate steps.

To insist on this view of causality would be overwhelming to most social scientists. The events we think of as effects usually occur after the events we think of as causes. There may be links we do not see in the chain, and maybe it would be a good thing to try to see them, to fill in the blanks, but often it is not feasible to do so. Besides that, we are primarily interested in finding successful interventions and although it would be nice to understand the mechanisms in the connection of two events, we often are willing to act without that information, just as physicians may use treatments because they work although they do not fully understand how. So an important element of our idea of causality is that cause must precede effect.

This is related to another philosophical issue; reductionism. In the view of some, explanations in one science theoretically can be reduced to explanations using the ideas of a more basic science. Thus sociological explanations should be reducible to psychological terms, thence to physiological, and so on until we get to the physics of elementary particles. Against this view is that of emergentism which holds, roughly speaking, that the whole is more than the sum of its parts. For example, what happens in social groups is not fully explainable by basic psychological principles, but rather requires new explanations.

Still another problem with the idea of the time order of cause and effect has to do with how much time lapses between the two. The longer the period of time between the supposed cause and effect, the more difficult it is to demonstrate the relationship. For example, demonstrating that smoking is a cause of lung cancer has been quite difficult because of the possibility of a latency period between the two events. In our conception of cause we will permit cause and effect to be separated by long time periods, but we recognize that the longer the time period, the more difficult it is to demonstrate causation.

Sufficiency. The insistence that in order to speak of A causing B we must have B occurring whenever A occurs creates difficulties for social science. Most of the cause-effect relationships with which we deal are not of this character; that is, only rarely do we have situations in which A is invariably followed by B. Often the most we can say is that B usually follows A, or the probability of B is greater if A has occurred than if it has not. Thus relationships between events are probabilistic. One of the objectives of research is to determine the probability that B will follow A.

The hard nosed scientist might insist that this appeal to probabilistic rather than deterministic causes is only an attempt to rationalize our ignorance. Instead of concluding with A causes B x percent of the time, we should work to specify the conditions under which A invariably causes B. Frequently we pursue this understanding, but it is rarely feasible to specify all the conditions for a causal connection and we are left with probabilistic statements.

Necessity. Again, to require that A always occur before B in order to talk of cause is unacceptable. Social phenomena are almost always multicausal. For example, mental illness may result from genetic deficiencies, physiological malfunctioning, disordered family life, or a number of other factors. Although ideally we may wish to know all of the causes of a particular effect, we will be quite happy to nail down one or two of them that we can use to effect change.

Multiple Occurrences. The statement of the conditions for cause implies that there is more than one occasion on which the successive occurrence of cause and effect are observed. It is difficult for us to explain an event that happens only once. For example, the first time men observed an eclipse of the sun it would have been hard for them to construct an accurate cause-effect explanation. Thus we will confine our concept of cause only to events that happen many times. Of course when faced with what seems to be a unique event we sometimes put it in a category with other events for which we do have explanations. Thus although World War II was a unique event, we might put it in the category of wars and this might help us understand it better. Similarly, early man might have classified an eclipse as a catastrophe, a category for which he might have an explanation.

Connecting Mechanisms. There are times when *B* almost invariably follows *A* but it just doesn't make sense to think of *A* as a cause of *B* (night always follows day but it doesn't make too much sense to think of day causing night). In physics it may be possible to see rather directly the mechanism by which a cause has an effect. In the social sciences, the connection is often much less obvious. However, since scientists have well-developed imaginations it is usually possible for them to construct explanations of cause-effect connections that appear to make sense and influence others to adopt their conclusions. We should be skeptical of such explanations, recognizing that they may function to provide psychological comfort rather than logical soundness. Nonetheless, we will require that the causal connection make sense.

SUMMARY OF OUR IDEA OF CAUSE

The concept of cause presented here includes the following elements: We will say that *A* is a cause of *B* if *A* preceeds *B* in time, if *B* is more likely when *A* has occurred and if there is a sensible link between *A* and *B*. We recognize that *B* probably has multiple causes. This notion of cause is no doubt too elementary for many philosophers, but it serves the practicing social scientist quite well.

Summary

In this chapter we considered more fully certain issues in the design of social research. The design specifies the unit of analysis, the sampling procedure, the variables on which information is to be obtained, the data collection and measurement procedures, and the plan for the analysis of data. It also specifies when data are to be collected in relation to the subjects' other experiences.

Studies of causal relationships require particular care in design. Problems that occur include the possibility that the cause-effect relationship is the reverse of our expectations, and that factors other than those in which we are interested account for the effect. The best way to eliminate (or control for) alternative explanations is through a rigorously controlled, randomized experimental design. Many times, however, experimental designs are not possible, and we are forced to try to control for alternative explanations through statistical analysis. These quasi-experimental designs require that we attempt to identify reasonable alternative explanations in advance. Categories of alternative explanations have been identified to help researchers think about these problems. These include random or chance factors, history, maturation, selection, mortality, regression, testing and measurement, and treatment contamination.

In addition to making judgments about causal connections within the particular study group, researchers are concerned with generalizing to a larger scale. This implicates the study's external validity. The best way to assure this is to study a random sample of the population to which we want to generalize. Again, this ideal often is not achieved and generalization must depend on reasoning and judgments.

This chapter ends with a discussion of the idea of causality. Various components of the concept were discussed including the idea of time precedence, sufficiency, necessity, multiple occurrence, and connecting mechanisms.

Notes

1. Donald T. Campbell and Julian C. Stanley, *Experimental and Quasi-Experimental Designs for Research*, Chicago: Rand McNally, 1963.
2. Thomas D. Cook and Donald T. Campbell, *Quasi-Experimentation: Design and Analysis Issues for Field Settings*, Chicago: Rand McNally, 1979.
3. *Ibid*.

Bibliography

Books on research design include:

Thomas D. Cook and Donald T. Campbell, *Quasi-Experimentation*, Chicago: Rand McNally, 1979.

Abraham Kaplan, *The Conduct of Inquiry*, San Francisco: Chandler, 1964.

Fred N. Kerlinger, *Foundations of Behavioral Research*, New York: Holt, Rinehart and Winston, 1964.

Donald T. Campbell and Julian C. Stanley, *Experimental and Quasi Experimental Designs for Research*, Chicago: Rand McNally, 1966.

10

Data Collection

There are two primary ways to find out things about people: ask them questions or observe them. Less direct ways include asking others about them or looking at records or things people have produced, like diaries or letters. In this chapter we are concerned with methods of questioning and observation.

Questionnaire Construction

A researcher can ask questions in writing (asking the person to fill out a self-administered questionnaire) or by interviewing (in person or over the phone). An interviewer is guided by a written set of questions and instructions called an *interview schedule*. In both of these situations the primary task is to figure out what questions to ask and how to ask them. Since the problems of constructing self-administered questionnaires and interview schedules are similar, we will talk about them both as matters of questionnaire construction.

There are few hard-and-fast rules for how to go about writing a questionnaire. Unlike some topics considered in this book, there is little logically derived theory for this process. There are rules of thumb, based largely on the experience of researchers. Most of these rules are *don'ts* rather than *dos*. That is, they are warnings against pitfalls, rather than rules for how to proceed.

Ideally, the questions should be derived logically from the formulation of the study although researchers seem to find reasons to ask some questions that are related only tangentially to the stated research problem. There is always more than one way to ask a question and the answers one gets depend very much on this factor.

There are two types of questions on questionnaires: fixed response and open ended. Fixed response questions require the respondent to choose an answer from a set of possible responses, for example:

"In terms of political orientation, would you say you are a:

1. liberal
2. moderate
3. conservative?"

Open-ended questions do not provide specific responses, instead they allow the respondent to answer freely. For example:

"What would you say your political orientation is?"

Some open ended questions require only very short answers and the possible answers are known before-hand, for example, "What is your age?" Other open ended questions are more truly open in the sense that we do not know what answers we are going to get when we write the question.

The advantage of fixed response questions is that all respondents answer within the same framework. Therefore answers are comparable from one respondent to another. Fixed response questions are often more reliable than open-ended ones because people are likely to respond the same way at different times. The disadvantage is that the available responses may not truly reflect the ideas of the respondents. The advantages of open-ended questions are the other side of the coin. They give much more latitude in response, permitting unique answers. Thus they may have greater validity in that they capture more accurately what the respondent thinks or feels.

Before analyzing responses to an open-ended questionnaire, it is necessary to code them in some way, that is, to categorize or scale them. Unlike open-ended questions which require a great deal of work, fixed response questions have the advantage of being precoded, the categories are already determined. For this reason, their use is preferred when the set of possible answers is known.

The response categories for fixed response questions must be mutually exclusive and exhaustive: They must not overlap and must take into account all possible responses. For this reason, an "other" category is sometimes included in the possible responses. These usually are not very informative, however, so the responses should be as exhaustive as possible to discourage this choice.

Some rules for writing questions are:

1. Most importantly, strive for clarity. Ambiguous words and phrasing, and words that have different meanings for different respondents should be avoided.
2. Use language that the respondents will understand. One would use different language in questionnaires aimed at college professors and street gang members. However, slang usually should be avoided, since its meaning may vary for different respondents and respondents may be offended by your use of it.
3. Questions should be short and to the point. Long questions will lose the respondent; he will forget the beginning and become frustrated or respond only to the last part of the question.
4. Ask only one question at a time. Questions with "and" or "or" are particularly suspicious. You would not ask: "Are you in favor of abortion and capital punishment?"
5. Questions must have answers the respondent can give. This may seem to be an obvious rule, but it is sometimes violated. Respondents shouldn't be asked for their opinions on things they have no opinion about. For example, most people have no opinion about the policy of the United States toward Burma, since they probably don't know what the policy is.
6. In general, do not ask leading questions, that is, questions that suggest what the answer should be. For example, "Are you in favor of President Reagan's policies on social security?" should be phrased, "Do you agree or disagree with the President's policies on social security?"

Some areas of inquiry are particularly affected by social desirability factors. That is, respondents will answer in ways they think are expected, rather than revealing their true feelings or behavior. An example is questions about behavior that society views negatively, like delinquent behavior or certain sexual behaviors. In areas such as this, questions must be phrased so as to counterbalance the social proscription.

SCALES

Many variables in the social sciences are measured by adding together responses to a set of questions. Examples are intelligence and achievement tests in which scores are computed on the basis of the number of right answers. Many other attitudes, behaviors, and traits are measured by similar means. Such measurement procedures are called *scales*. Scales come in many varieties. Usually they are made up of a series of questions that all have the same format. For example, one might reveal attitudes toward social science research by presenting respondents with a series of assertions about research and asking them whether they agree or disagree. A summated scale is formed by adding up the responses to a series of these questions. We might assign a value of one to a response of agree and zero to disagree and then add up these numbers for all items. Degree of agreement or disagreement might be obtained also, as in the following example:
"Social science researchers only study the obvious.

1. Strongly agree
2. Agree
3. Disagree
4. Strongly disagree."

Or the respondent might be asked to check his position along a continuum as in Figure 10.1. In both cases numbers can be assigned to each possible response and the chosen responses

FIGURE 10.1

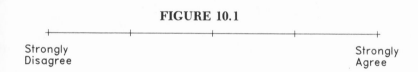

Strongly   Strongly
Disagree   Agree

added up for each subject. Variables that are constructed using degree questions such as this are called *Likert scales*. A refinement of Likert scaling is *Guttman* scaling. In Guttman scaling the series of items have some order; that is, if a person agrees with a particular question he will also agree with all of the questions higher up in the order. Guttman scales are much more difficult to construct, but they have the advantage of assuring that the measurement is unidimensional, that is, that a single concept is being measured.

One of the problems with multi-item scales is the tendency to respond to a set of items in a fixed or stereotypical manner. This is known as a *response set*. For example, some people tend to agree with everything without discriminating among the questions. Scales should be constructed to minimize response sets as much as possible. Wording some questions positively and some negatively helps break up stereotypical responding. (Of course, the responses to negative questions must be recoded—reversed—before adding them to positive questions.) Sometimes exactly the same question is asked with the wording reversed at different places in the questionnaire to check the reliability of responses.

A great many scales have been developed and are available for use in social research. Recently a series of nine easily administered scales for use in clinical work has been developed by Walter Hudson.[1] These scales each have twenty-five statements. Respondents are asked whether the statement applies to them most or all of the time, a good part of the time, some of the time, a little of the time or rarely, or none of the time. The scales include measures of nonpsychotic depression, self-esteem, marital satisfaction, sexual satisfaction, discord between children and their parents, family stress, and peer relations. An example of an item on the nonpsychotic depression scale is: "I feel powerless to do anything about my life." Other scales that are particularly useful for social work research and evaluation may be found in the works in the bibliography to this chapter.

It is often necessary to develop scales specifically for the particular research. Individualized scales can even be developed for work with a single individual. These can be administered at several times during treatment to help determine change. For example, if one is working with a woman to help her be more assertive in her social relationships, one might develop a scale based on a series of situations she faces in which she allows others to push her around.

PROJECTIVE METHODS

Projective methods are measurement procedures used to get a subject to reveal things about himself he is unlikely to reveal in response to direct questions. Projective techniques involve asking the subject to respond to ambiguous stimuli. For example, subjects might be asked to describe what they see in a series of inkblots (the Rorschach test) or to tell stories about a series of ambiguous pictures of people (as in the Thematic Apperception Test). Projective test stimuli can also be verbal as in the Minnesota Multiphasic Inventory (the MMPI). In theory, people will project their feelings and even their unconscious impulses onto the stimuli.

A great deal of controversy surrounds the use of projective tests. Advocates assert that they are useful for diagnosing psychological problems and for revealing the structure of the unconscious. Skeptics point out that the interpretation of projective responses requires a great deal of inference. Interpretations by different experts are often quite different, hence the reliability of such techniques is often low. The validity of projective tests also can be questioned since some investigators doubt that people really do reveal themselves on such tests. In any event, projective techniques should be used only after considerable study. They are sometimes useful in conjunction with other types of measures which may serve to confirm the outcome.

PRETESTING

An essential step in developing any questionnaire or other instrument is the pretest. This involves administering the questionnaire to a group of persons who will not be in the main study sample. Persons selected for the pretest should be similar to those who will eventually be studied. This step serves to uncover problems in the questionnaire (such as unclear wording) and suggests ways to revise the instrument so that it is easier for respondents. Pretest respondents should be encouraged to be critical and their reactions, both overall and specific should be sought.

Sometimes instruments are given a preliminary testing for other reasons as well, for example, to further develop scales. This is done by means of an item analysis and requires many more respondents than pretesting for clarity of wording. Usually the preliminary version of a scale contains items that should be eliminated. Those that have very little variation in response (items that most people answer in the same way) usually should be dropped. The relationship of items to each other and to the full scale are examined to locate those that do not fit. Dropping them will improve the reliability of the scale. Initial reliability can be checked and perhaps more elaborate analyses, such as factor analysis performed.

QUESTIONNAIRES VERSUS INTERVIEWS

In the course of a research project, one often has to decide whether to use self-administered questionnaires or personal interviews. Questionnaires are more anonymous, less expensive in staff time, and provide for more standardization of the stimulus. The disadvantages include the possibility that respondents may postpone them, fail to complete them, or leave out questions. In addition, one does not have a chance to explain questions. With interviews one may get more information, since it is harder to turn down an interviewer and harder to ignore questions. In addition, an interviewer can explain unclear questions. Interviews, however, are much more expensive than questionnaires.

Observation

The most common method scientists use to understand the world is observation. Direct observation of human behavior is the principal data collection method in much social science research, including anthropological studies of cultures, sociological studies of organizational functioning, and studies of family interaction. In this section we consider the use of observation in the evaluation of intervention with particular emphasis on single case studies.

Work with an individual case often involves efforts to change the behavior of the client in some way. We hope to increase or decrease the occurrence of certain actions. Evaluation of such work is concerned with determining whether or not the desired change has taken place. As indicated earlier, this usually involves measurement of the behavior at several points, both before and after intervention efforts are instituted. The observations must be structured and systematized to assure reliability and consistency over time.

The most important element in an observational scheme is the definition of the behavior of interest. This must be clear and unambiguous so the observer can be confident that he knows whether or not a behavior has occurred. For example, if our task is to increase the social interaction of a withdrawn patient on a psychiatric ward, we must be able to define exactly what we mean by social interaction. Does it mean merely approaching another person or having eye contact with him, or must the patient attempt to talk with the other person? Must the other person respond to the patient? The definitions of the behaviors of interest are called *behavioral codes*. Codes are often tailored to the particular case and frequently are refined and made more precise as the study progresses.

In developing observational schemes for behaviors it may be useful to distinguish among the frequency of a behavior, the duration of each occurence and its strength or severity. Sometimes only one of these factors changes. For example, a child's temper tantrums may not decrease in frequency but may become shorter and less severe. This outcome would not be found if only frequency were measured.[2]

Ordinarily we can not watch people all the time so specific time periods are sampled. Our psychiatric patient might be observed from one o'clock to two o'clock every afternoon. Recording of behaviors usually occurs in one of two ways. Either each behavior is recorded when it occurs or time is divided into short intervals (for example, 10 second intervals) and whether or not the behavior occurs in each is noted. The first method is often used for relatively infrequent behaviors while the second is used for more common behaviors. In interval recording the length of the interval is determined by the frequency of the behavior. We want the intervals to be short enough so it is unlikely that the behavior will occur more than once in one interval.

When each occurrence is recorded, a summary count (frequency) for the period of the observations is used in the subsequent analysis. When interval recording is used the number of intervals in which the behavior occurred is counted.

RELIABILITY

The accuracy of observational data is checked by utilizing two observers for at least some (a sample) of the observational periods. Ideally two observers should be used for all of the data collection but that is rarely feasible. The extent of agreement between the two indicates the data's reliability. Degree of agreement may be calculated in several ways. For data in which behavior is present or absent, the usual procedure is to count the number of instances in which either or both observers thought the behavior occurred. Percentage of agreement is computed as the number of agreements divided by the total and multiplied by 100. For example, suppose we are observing interactions of a patient on a psychiatric ward. At the end of each minute two observers note whether the patient has interacted with others during that time. Observation goes on for one hour. Suppose the data from the two observers looked like Table 10.1. One or both of the observers thought interaction occurred in twenty-five of the time periods and they agreed on twenty of those periods. Hence the reliability is 20/25 times 100 or 80 percent. Data in which the percentage of agreement exceeds 80 percent is generally thought to be reliable.

Although this procedure has become generally accepted, some analysts have objected on the grounds that it fails to account for the agreement expected by chance. If raters were to make their judgments randomly, without any attention to behavior, they would, merely by chance, agree a certain proportion of the time.

TABLE 10.1

Observer 2	Observer 1		
	Interaction	No Interaction	Total
Interaction	20	3	23
No interaction	2	35	37
Total	22	38	60

How much chance agreement can be expected depends on the distribution of the data, that is, how frequently the behavior occurs. If it is very frequent, observers will tend to agree more often on its occurrence. Some measures are available to correct for (or subtract out) such chance agreements.[3]

Sometimes a lower percentage of agreement is obtained if the calculations are based on nonoccurrence rather than occurrence. This will happen if the behavior occurs the majority of the time. It has become accepted practice to quote the lower of the two possible percents of agreement.

Unfortunately high percentages of agreement do not necessarily guarantee good data. Many studies have shown that coders tend to be more reliable during reliability check periods than at other times. In addition, reliability often tends to deteriorate over time. For that reason, it is important to check it at several points during the course of a study.

TRAINING OF OBSERVERS

It is crucial that considerable time and effort be expended in training observers. They should be instructed carefully in the meanings of the behavioral codes and given the opportunity to practice coding before actual data collection begins. Ideally, their reliability should be assured before gathering actual data. Retraining may be necessary if reliability deteriorates later on. If reliability is bad the researcher must consider the possibility that the code is badly defined.

In studies of intervention using observations, people usually know they are being observed (most often it is unethical to deceive them on this point). However, they may behave differently when they are being watched than they do when alone or with family or friends. The investigator must be aware of the possible effects of observation on behavior, particularly when the observer is intrusive (for example, when he or she comes during the evening to sit in a corner of the living room). Sometimes the problem is reduced by allowing the individual or family to get used to (become habituated to) the presence of the observer.

Electronic recording devices (audio and video recorders) are being used more and more in the investigation of therapeutic interventions. Such devices also have an impact on the behavior of persons although some research indicates the impact may be less than therapists imagine, particularly after clients get used to them.

SELF REPORT

Increasingly, clients are being used as observers of their own or family members' behavior. They can be trained to use observational codes and record the occurrence of behaviors. Client self-report is often used because of the costs of other observers. In addition, some workers view it as an integral part of the intervention process; the experience of observational training and self-observation can help in achieving change. Balancing these benefits is the fact that many clients find observational procedures such as counting behaviors and filling out forms to be onerous. As a result they may neglect the data gathering requirements on some days and thus jeopardize the completion of the research. Or they might just drop out of treatment. It is usually desirable to make self-report requirements as unobtrusive as possible.

With self-report the problem of reactivity to the measurement may be particularly acute. People may change their behavior because they are paying attention to it and having to record it. For example, a person may decrease cigarette consumption when he has to record each cigarette smoked. Such reactivity can be used for therapeutic benefit, but it lessens the usefulness of self-report for research purposes.

As with other coders, the reliability of client self-report should be checked by having an independent observer present for some of the observational periods. Generally, agreement between observer and client is not as high as between two independent observers since the former pair look at the situation in different ways, and have different stakes in the outcome.

Summary

This chapter has been concerned with the problems of questionnaire construction (either self-administered or interviewing questionnaires) and observation. Questionnaires consist of either open-ended or fixed response questions. Often variables are measured by sets of questions which are then combined. Questions should be short and clear, written in language that is easily understood by respondents. When writing questionnaires we must recognize that results may be colored by the social desirability of responses and response sets. The pretest is an essential part of the development of a questionnaire.

Observation is one of the most common procedures for collecting data in all sciences. In this chapter we considered the use of observation in studies of work with individual cases. Such studies are usually concerned with the observation of overt behavior (which may include verbalizations and other communication). Careful definition of the behavior of interest is required and the reliability of observations should be evaluated.

Notes

1. Walter W. Hudson, *The Clinical Measurement Package: A Field Manual*, Homewood, Il.: Dorsey Press, 1982.
2. Glenn R. Green, *Modification of Verbal Behavior of the Impaired Elderly*, unpublished Ph.D. dissertation, The University of Chicago, June 1982.
3. R. Light, Measures of Response Agreement for Qualitative Data, *Psychological Bulletin*, 76:365-377, 1971.

Bibliography

The following books include measuring instruments of use to human services professionals:

Graham B. Spanier, Measuring Dyadic Adjustment: New Scales for Assessing the Quality of Marriage and Similar Dyads, *Journal of Marriage and the Family*, 38:15-28, 1976

Oscar Krisen Buros, Ed., *The Eighth Mental Measurements Yearbook*, Highland Park, N.J.: Gryphon Press, 1978.

Walter W. Hudson, *The Clinical Measurement Package: A Field Manual*, Homewood, Il.: Dorsey Press, 1982.

The following include additional discussions of measurment:

Michel Hersen and David H. Barlow, *Single Case Experimental Designs*, New York: Pergamon Press, 1976.

Srnika Jayaratne and Rona L. Levy, *Empirical Clinical Practice*, New York: Columbia University Press, 1979.

11

Measurement

In Chapter 2 we defined reliability in terms of the extent of random error in measurements. Here we discuss this idea more extensively and talk about how reliability is measured.

Reliability

As mentioned in Chapter 2 the determination of the reliability of a measure depends on obtaining two or more measures of the same thing and seeing how closely they agree. Psychometricians (scientists concerned with constructing psychological measures) originally developed the idea of reliability in the context of studies of groups of people. These studies were concerned with the construction of intelligence and achievement tests. They developed two principal ways of determining reliability called *repeated measures reliability* (often called test-retest reliability) and *internal consistency reliability*.

REPEATED MEASURES RELIABILITY

Repeated measures reliability refers to the situation in which we apply exactly the same measurement operations at two times to the same group of people. The two times should be fairly close together. If the measure is reliable, an individual's score should be about the same each time. More important from a researcher's point of view is that the order of people assessed should be the same or as similar as possible on both occasions and there should be about the same interval between people on the two applications of the measure. When this is the case we say that the applications of the measure are highly associated. If, on the other hand, the measure is not reliable (if it has lots of error in it), the values for people will tend not to be the same at each measurement, and people will tend to be switched around in their order on the measure. The two applications will not be associated very highly.

Statisticians have developed lots of measures of association. The one most often used in estimating reliability is called the correlation coefficient (also called the product moment correlation coefficient or the Pearson r). We have more to say about the correlation coefficient in the next chapter. Repeated measures reliability is estimated by the correlation between the two applications of the measure. This correlation is sometimes called the test-retest reliability coefficient. In this context the correlation will be a fraction (or decimal) between zero and one. The fraction represents the proportion of the observed variance that is due to real variation in the characteristic being measured. We have considered here the case in which we have only two applications of the measure. It is better, though rare, to have more than two. In that case, the ideas are the same but the statistical analysis is more complicated.

One of the problems encountered in repeated measures reliability is the question of how much time should elapse between the two measurements. The answer to this question depends on the nature of the measure. On the one hand, one does not want to allow so much time to pass that the value of the variable actually changes. If that were to occur, the correlation coefficient would be measuring both reliability and extent of change in the variable itself, and it would be impossible to sort out the two. On the other hand, some measures (such as intelligence tests and attitude questionnaires) may be affected by memory. If the time is too short between the two administrations of the measure, people may remember it, and their responses may be affected by that memory. Thus influenced, they would give the same answer or a different one if they thought they had figured out a better answer. In this case, the correlation coefficient would be measuring the effects of memory as well as random error. The determination of the length of time between measures is a matter of balancing these two considerations. Other factors such as feasibility and cost often affect this decision as well.

INTERNAL CONSISTENCY RELIABILITY

Measures, such as intelligence tests or psychological inventories are made up of lots of items, and a person's score or value is determined by adding up the responses. When this is the case it is possible to think of reliability in terms of the internal consistency of the items: to what extent are the responses similar? The simplest form of internal consistency reliability is called *odd-even* or *split-half* reliability. We divide the items in two (perhaps by taking every other one) and treat the parts as if they were two separate, but nearly identical measures. We then have two values for each respondent (the sum of these two values is the value for the total measure). If the measure is reliable, these two sets of scores should be highly associated. We compute the correlation between these values over the entire group of respondents; this is the split-half reliability of the measure. Actually it is the reliability of either half of the measure. A simple adjustment is made to estimate the reliability of the total score.

The idea of split-half reliability can be elaborated to provide more elegant measures of internal consistency. Taking every other item is just one way to divide the items into subtests. A more sophisticated approach to reliability is to get an average of all the correlations we would get from all possible pairs of subtests within a measure.

Even when we have a test or measurement with many items,

there are often limitations to the application of internal consistency reliability. Sometimes we have measures that are not intended to be internally consistent. For example, a measure of general psychological health might have items on which we would not expect to have a consistency of response. We might have no reason to expect that an item tapping depression would be related to an item tapping neurotic tendencies. Hence there are some multi-item measures for which a measure of internal consistency is not appropriate.

JUDGE OR RATER RELIABILITY

Many of the measurements used in social work and social science research consist of judgements or ratings. For example in a study of the effectiveness of casework in a family service agency, we might have judges rate the amount of movement or change in the case from its opening to its closing. In this instance the usual approach to reliability is to have at least two observers rate the same thing on at least a sample of cases. A measure of the amount of agreement between the observers is made in the form of a correlation coefficient, the percentage of ratings on which the observers agree, or some other measure of association, depending on the nature of the data.

The idea behind this approach to the reliability of ratings is that there are random errors involved in the observers' methods. Thus the association among ratings made by two or more judges should estimate their reliability. It would seem that this is merely an extension of the ideas behind test-retest and split-half reliability to the rating situation. Unfortunately, matters are not that simple. Disagreements among raters may be due to factors that are not random, but systematic. For example, disagreement may be due to differences in the way in which raters interpret the instructions they are given or differences in the way they interpret the behavior of subjects. Since such differences are not random, they may be thought of as validity considerations.

When working with ratings it is important to obtain, whenever possible, a measure of interrater agreement. We refer to this here as interrater reliability but we recognize that such measures of agreement capture elements of both reliability and validity.

THE THEORY OF RELIABILITY

In this section we develop the theoretical basis for the notion of reliability, again depending on ideas from psychometrics. We will focus primarily on variables that have numerical values, although the argument can be adapted to categorical variables as well. We begin with the idea that a particular individual has a true value for a particular variable. Measurement is concerned with estimating that true value and minimizing the degree of random error. The estimated or observed value can be written as:

$$x_o = x_t + x_e$$

where x_o is the observed value, x_t is the true (but unknown) value and x_e is an error caused by random fluctuations. The value x_e can be either positive or negative, so the observed value may be above or below the true value.

If we were to make several observations of the same variable for an individual within a short period of time we would expect the true value to stay the same but the error component would differ for each observation and the observed value would vary. The observed values will be above and below the true value in similar proportions, as shown in Figure 11.1. If the measurement has a lot of error in it the observed values will be scattered widely around the true value, as shown in Figure 11.2. If there isn't much error the observed values will be clustered around the true value as in Figure 11.3. We would say that the observed values in Figure 11.3 are more reliable than those in Figure 11.2.

One of the ways of thinking about reliability is in terms of how much scatter or variation there is in observed values (assuming that the true value is in the middle of the observed values). Statisticians have developed a number of ways of measuring the

FIGURE 11.1

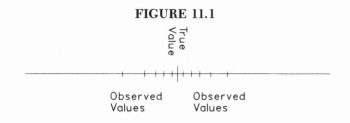

Observed   Observed
Values   Values

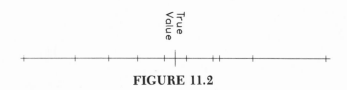

FIGURE 11.2

amount of variation in observations. We discuss these in Chapter 12. One measure of variation is called the variance. We could compare the two measurements in Figures 11.2 and 11.3 for the amount of error they have in them (and thus their reliability) by comparing the variances of the observed values.

Although the above is a good way to begin to think about reliability, in actual practice it does not provide us with a way of determining the reliability of measurements. We usually are not in a position to take a number of observations on the same individual within a short period of time. The situation we are in more often is one of taking one or two observations on a number of individuals or several observations on one person over a longer period of time. (If we take observations over a long period of time we expect them to vary because of real changes in the variable.)

Psychometricians have developed the idea of reliability for use when studying a relatively large group of individuals. The true values of that group of individuals will vary, as will the observed values. It turns out that if the error is random, the variation in observed values will be greater than the variation in true values. In fact, if the variations are measured in terms of variances (the measure of variation mentioned above), the variance in the observed values is equal to the variance of the true values plus the variance due to random errors. This is written:

$$\sigma_o^2 = \sigma_t^2 + \sigma_e^2$$

where the Greek, lower case sigma σ with a square on it represents a variance. Thus σ_o^2 means the observed variance, σ_t^2 means the true variance, and σ_e^2 means the error variance. It should be

FIGURE 11.3

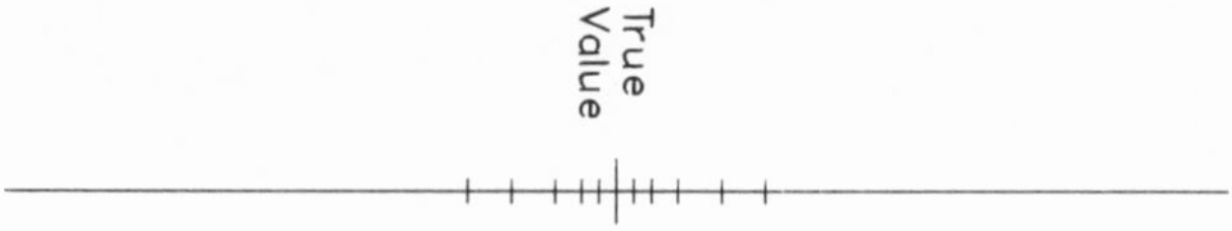

remembered that this equation refers to variations in values from lots of individuals. It is, however, similar to the earlier equation for a single individual.

The situation might be diagrammed as in Figure 11.4, where the whole bar represents the total variance in the observations and the divisions represent the true and error components.

Since the total observed variance in a set of values is the sum of the variance due to real differences among individuals plus the variance due to random error, it is possible to talk about the proportion of the total observed variance that is due to real differences. This proportion is considered to be the reliability of the measurement. It is written as follows:

$$r_{tt} = \frac{\sigma_t^2}{\sigma_o^2}$$

where r_{tt} means the reliability of the measure. Because the real variance is equal to the observed variance minus the error variance, the fraction is sometimes written as:

$$r_{tt} = \frac{\sigma_o^2 - \sigma_e^2}{\sigma_o^2}$$

If the bar in Figure 11.4 were considered to have an area of one, then parts of the bar would represent proportions of the total variance. Thus the area representing the true variance would be the reliability of the measure as indicated in Figure 11.5.

We still have not reached the point at which we can determine the actual reliability of a measure. That is, we cannot directly apply the above equation to find a value for r_{tt}. If we take only one measurement on a number of individuals we will be able

FIGURE 11.4

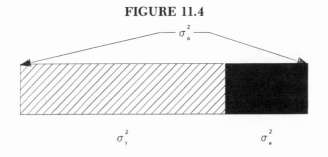

r_{tt} $1 - r_{tt}$

FIGURE 11.5

to determine only the variance in the observed values (the σ_o^2 in the above equation). To solve for r_{tt} we also need to know either σ_t^2 or σ_e^2.

The only way to begin to estimate r_{tt} is to have at least two measurements of the same thing on the same individuals. We then determine the association between the sets of measures and use it to estimate the reliability coefficient. The measure of association most often used is the correlation coefficient. We compute either the correlation between two halves of a test (internal consistency reliability) or the correlation between two administrations of a test (repeated measures or test-retest reliability) and consider the results reliability coefficients.

Validity

As indicated earlier, the validity of a measurement is limited by its reliability since, in theory, validity cannot exceed the square root of the reliability. We hope that some of the reliable part of a measure is valid; that is, that it predicts other things, is related to other things, or reflects some real underlying concept. This is shown by extending the diagrams of the previous section, as in Figure 11.6, where σ_v^2 is the valid part of the measurement.

FIGURE 11.6

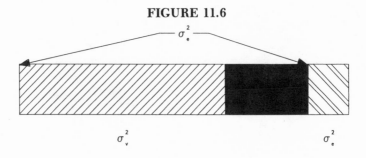

σ_v^2 σ_e^2

We can never know the reliability of a measure precisely, we can only estimate it. It is even harder to determine the validity of a measure. In fact, it is usually impossible to come up with a single number that represents the estimated validity of a measure. As indicated in Chapter 2, there are various ways to think about validity, some of which lend themselves to empirical investigation. These will be discussed below.

Criterion Validity. Criterion validity is the relationship of a measure to a well-defined criterion. The criterion itself should have obvious or well-established validity or the relationship between it and the measure will reflect invalid aspects of both. There are two subtypes of criterion validity. The first is concurrent validity, in which the criterion is measured at the same time as the measurement of interest. For example, an achievement test might be compared with current grades in a course. The second type of criterion validity is predictive validity in which the criterion is measured at some time after the measurement of interest. For example, aptitude test scores might be compared with school achievement in the year following the measurement. The usual index of criterion validity is the correlation coefficient. The square of the correlation coefficient indicates the proportion of variance that the two variables have in common, so we could represent criterion validity as in Figure 11.7 where r_{xy} indicates the correlation between the measure (x) and the criterion (y), and the square of the correlation, r_{xy}^2 is the valid variance of the measure (the variance associated with the criterion).

Discriminant Validity. Discriminant validity is similar to criterion validity. In discriminant validity we are asking whether a

FIGURE 11.7

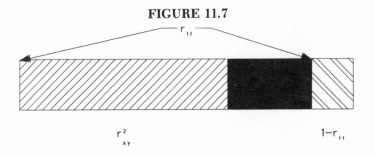

$$r_{xy}^2 \qquad\qquad 1-r_{tt}$$

measure can distinguish among two or more groups of people. The groups may be clearly and objectively defined, for example, people who complete a job training program and those who do not. Alternatively, the groups may be formed on the basis of judgment, for example, on the basis of psychiatric diagnoses of depression or schizophrenia. The simplest index of the validity of the measure is the proportion of cases the measurement correctly identifies. Other indices of discriminant validity, similar to the correlation coefficient, also are available.

Construct Validity. Construct validity is concerned with the relationship of a measure to measures of other concepts. As such, it depends on a relatively well-developed theory which specifies what the relationships among concepts should be. One of the most useful formulations of construct validity was advanced by Campbell and Fiske[1] who suggested that construct validity consists of two components: convergent and discriminant validity. A measure should have a relatively high association with some concepts (convergent validity) but should be practically unrelated to others (discriminant validity).

Factorial Validity. The idea of factorial validity is usually applied to measures which are made up of several elements or items, for example, symptom check lists, multi-item attitude scales, and school tests. Sometimes we think of such measuring instruments as reflecting one or more underlying components or factors. For example, we might construct a psychiatric rating scale with items designed to reveal aspects of depression and schizophrenia. The underlying components are sometimes called *dimensions*. If the measurement has only one factor it is called *unidimensional*. If it has two or more factors it is *multidimensional*.

A fairly complex set of statistical techniques known as *factor analysis* is used to determine how many dimensions a measure has and to identify the factors. These techniques can be used to confirm the intended dimensionality of a measure. Essentially, factor analysis identifies sets of items within a measure that tend to go together. Usually such items have relatively high intercorrelations among themselves and lower correlations with other items. Each item is thought of as reflecting one or more, but not all, of the underlying components (unless it is a unidemensional

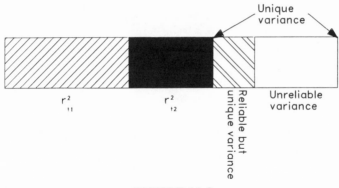

FIGURE 11.8

measure). In addition, each of the items has a unique or specific part that is unrelated to any of the components. The situation might be diagrammed as in Figure 11.8 which shows a measure with two factors F_1 and F_2. Thus, r_{t1} and r_{t2} are the correlations of the measure with F_1 and F_2, respectively.

Summary

In this chapter the theoretical foundations of reliability and validity of measures were examined somewhat more extensively than in previous chapters. The measurement of reliability and validity requires the calculation of measures of association. Three types of reliability were described. Repeated measures reliability is concerned with the stability of measures over relatively short periods of time. Internal consistency reliability applies to multi-item measures where responses are aggregated to form a score. Reliability indicates the extent to which the items are consistent in their attempt to measure a given quality. Judge or rater reliability is used when the measuring instrument involves a person's judgments; the reliability is determined by the extent of agreement among two or more judges.

Validity is determined by the relationship of a measure to measures of other things. Types of validity include criteria (concurrent and predictive), discriminant, construct, and factorial. The first two are oriented to the practical aspects of the measure while the last two are more concerned with theoretical issues.

The determination of reliability and validity may be thought of as attempts to understand the sources of the variance in observed values of a variable. Part of that variance is usually random error (the unreliable part); part is reliable but unique, that is, unrelated to other variables; and part is (we hope) valid. Sometimes we can divide the valid part further into two or more factors.

Notes

1. Donald T. Campbell and Donald W. Fiske, Convergent and Discriminant Validity by the Multitrait-Multimethod Matrix, *Psychological Bulletin*, 56:81-105, 1959.
2. John R. Schuerman, *Multivariate Analysis in the Human Services*, Boston: Kluwer-Nijhoff, 1983.

Bibliography

Important references on measurement include:

Anne Anastasi, *Psychological Testing*, New York: Macmillan, 1968.

L. J. Cronbach, Coefficient Alpha and the Internal Structure of Tests, *Psychometrika*, 16(3)297-334, 1951.

Donald W. Fiske, *Measuring the Concepts of Personality*, Chicago: Aldine, 1971.

J. P. Guilford, *Psychometric Methods*, New York: McGraw Hill, 1954.

J. C. Nunnally, *Psychometric Theory*, New York: McGraw Hill, 1978.

Warren S. Torgerson, *Theory and Methods of Scaling*, New York: Wiley, 1967.

D. K. Whitla Ed., *Handbook of Measurement and Assessment in Behavioral Science*, Reading, Ma.: Addison-Wesley, 1968.

12

Data Analysis

In earlier chapters we discussed some issues of data analysis particularly relevant to specific designs. Here we consider data analysis somewhat more extensively, although the discussion still is limited. A student intending to do social research must devote considerable study to statistics.

This chapter concerns the analysis of data from group designs. Statistical analyses can be categorized according to the number of variables involved. An analysis involving only one variable is called a *univariate analysis*, a two variable analysis is called *bivariate*, and an analysis involving more than two variables is called *multivariate*. Most research today involves all three types of analysis. In this chapter we concentrate on univariate and bivariate procedures and touch only briefly on multivariate techniques.

In this chapter please note that SPSS is a trademark of SPSS, Inc. of Chicago, IL for its proprietary computer software. No material describing such software may be produced or distributed without the written permission of SPSS, Inc.

Levels of Measurement

A critical concept in data analysis is the idea of levels of measurement. We will be concerned with three levels of measurement: categorical (or nominal), ordinal, and equal interval.

A *categorical* variable is one whose values are only categories. Examples are gender (male and female) and marital status (single, married, separated, divorced, and widowed). The values or categories of these variables have no meaningful order to them. Numbers represent the categories when computers are used to analyze the data. For example, males may be coded as one and females as zero. Such numbers are only codes and have none of the other meanings of numbers (it is not legitimate to add or multiply them).

Ordinal variables have values which have some order. A familiar example is attitudes toward something; for example, attitudes toward social work research could be measured on a scale with five ordered values: very favorable, somewhat favorable, indifferent, somewhat unfavorable, and very unfavorable. Level of social functioning or degree of involvement in an organization might also be ordinal scales.

Sometimes a distinction is made between two sub-types of ordinal variables: ordinal categories and ranked data. In ordinal categories we have a relatively small number of groups which have some meaningful order. In ranked data we rank all of the cases from high to low or low to high. For example, if we have a class of twenty-five students we might rank them from one to twenty-five on the basis of their ability in the subject. Usually, ranked data contains ties. Two or more students might be indistinguishable in ability and thus would receive the same rank. Ordinal categories can be thought of as ranked data with lots of ties, so the distinction between these subtypes gets blurred. Nonetheless, these subcategories of ordinal variables lead to slightly different analytic procedures.

Usually, the categories of ordinal variables are coded with numbers (for example, very favorable equals 1, somewhat favorable equals 2). The order of the numbers gives the order of the categories but no assumptions are made about the distances between categories. That is, the difference between categories one and two is not necessarily the same as the difference between categories two and three.

The third level of measurement is called equal interval or simply interval. *Interval* variables are ordered variables in which the distances between values have meaning. Furthermore, the distance between 2 and 3 is the same as the distance between 3 and 4. Examples of interval variables are age, number of days between hospitalizations, and number of arrests.

Equal interval variables are either continuous or discontinuous. A *continuous* variable is one in which it is possible to have any fractional value between any two other values (for example, age is a continuous variable since time can be divided into increments as small as we wish). A *discontinuous* variable is one that can only take certain values. Counts of things are always discontinuous. For example, we can't have 2.5 children in a family. (Although it is meaningful to talk about a group of families having an average of 2.5 children.) A variable that is inherently continuous is always measured in a discontinuous way; that is, there is always a limit to the precision with which we can measure things. For example, in a particular study age might be measured only to the nearest year, ignoring months, days, hours, seconds, and fractions of seconds.

Still a fourth level of measurement is sometimes identified: the ratio scale. A *ratio* scale is an interval scale in which there is a natural zero, a point at which the characteristic is not present. The examples of interval scales above are also ratio scales. With ratio scales we can talk about the ratio of two values; that is, we can talk about one person having been out of the hospital two and a half times as long as another person.

It is important to distinguish levels of measurement in order to use appropriate statistical procedures. For example, procedures that are valid for equal interval data may not be valid for categorical data. The levels of measurement themselves form an ordinal scale consisting of:

1. Categorical (low)
2. Ordinal
3. Equal interval (high)

Statistical procedures that are valid for lower level variables are also valid for higher level variables, but the reverse is not true. There is one exception to this rule. It turns out that interval level techniques may sometimes be used with categorical variables having only two categories (called *dichotomous* variables or *dichotomies*.

The rules for the validity of particular techniques at particular levels of measurement come from the logic and mathematics of the techniques. The rules often are violated in practice. In particular, techniques appropriate for equal interval variables are often used with ordinal variables. There has been much debate and some research on the effects of violations of these rules. There are circumstances in which using equal interval techniques on ordinal variables does not lead to serious errors of interpretation. This is particularly true when ordinal variables are thought of as being inherently equal interval. This means the characteristics being measured are thought of as equal interval although the imperfect way we measure them produces only ordinal variables.

Descriptive Statistics

The first task of data analysis is one of description. We begin by describing the important characteristics of the study group one at a time (univariate descriptive statistics) and then go on to describe the relationships among these characteristics (bivariate or multivariate descriptive statistics).

We start with a list of the values on each variable for our subjects. Suppose that I have done a study of married women who were discharged from a psychiatric hospital. Four of the variables in the study are race-ethnicity, age, level of social functioning, and socioeconomic status (S.E.S.). There are persons from three racial-ethnic groups in the study, coded as follows: 1 equals white, 2 equals black and 3 equals hispanic. Level of social functioning is a variable constructed by adding together a number of items measuring performance in various areas of functioning. It may be considered an ordinal variable with values ranging from zero to ten. Socioeconomic status is an ordinal variable with values from one to five based on educational attainment and occupation. We have twenty-five cases in our study, and the values of the cases on these four variables are shown in Table 12.1.

This listing of values constitutes a complete description of the group in regard to the four variables. However it is difficult to read and get a sense of what the group is like. It would be even

TABLE 12.1

Case Number	Race	Age	Level of Social Functioning	S.E.S.
1	1	32	7	1
2	2	25	3	3
3	2	35	1	5
4	1	22	0	3
5	2	33	6	2
6	1	20	3	2
7	3	24	8	5
8	2	62	6	5
9	1	23	4	3
10	1	59	5	3
11	2	55	5	4
12	1	40	3	4
13	1	18	1	4
14	3	37	4	5
15	1	28	0	2
16	1	33	2	3
17	1	23	1	4
18	3	35	2	5
19	2	23	3	5
20	1	51	9	4
21	1	63	6	4
22	1	42	1	1
23	1	29	2	4
24	1	44	7	4
25	2	39	0	5

harder to read if we had many more cases. If it were rearranged so the values ran from low to high—for example, if the cases were listed in order of age—the information might be understood more easily. However, we need more efficient ways of summarizing the data so they are more easily understood.

FREQUENCY DISTRIBUTIONS

The simplest univariate descriptive technique is called *frequency distribution*. This is a listing of each of the values of a variable together with the number of cases with each value. For example, a frequency distribution of race-ethnicity for the above data would look like that shown in Table 12.2. Sometimes we add

**TABLE 12.2   Frequency
Distribution of Race–
Ethnicity**

Code	Value	Number
1	White	15
2	Black	7
3	Hispanic	3
	Total	25

another column to a frequency distribution table giving the percentage of cases in each category, as in Table 12.3. This is a frequency distribution table for a categorical variable. A frequency distribution for an equal interval variable or an ordinal variable with many values would be quite long. It might even have almost as many values as cases. A frequency distribution of the variable age in our example would have twenty-one values, so it would not summarize very much. For that reason, we usually collapse equal interval variables into a smaller number of categories, each having several values of the variable. A collapsed frequency distribution of age looks like the information found in Table 12.4. The last column in Table 12.4 (the cumulative percent) sometimes appears on frequency distributions of interval and ordinal data. It shows the percentage of cases at or below each value.

Obviously one can collapse an equal interval variable in several ways. There are at least four different approaches:

1. Use natural or theoretically significant categories. For example, age might have the categories 0-18, 19-64, and 65 and above.
2. Use break points of the distribution. This approach requires that we first examine the full distribution. We look for gaps in it and use them as the boundaries for our categories.
3. Divide the group into categories with equal numbers of cases.

TABLE 12.3

Code	Value	Number	%
1	White	15	60
2	Black	7	28
3	Hispanic	3	12
	Total	25	100

TABLE 12.4

Age	Number	%	Cumulative %
Below 30	10	40	40
30–39	7	28	68
40–49	3	12	80
50 and above	5	20	100
Total	25	100	

This means we select the boundaries for our categories so each group has the same or nearly the same numbers of cases in them. Sometimes researchers use four categories; these are called quartiles.

4. Divide the scale into equal lengths. For example 0-9, 10-19, 20-29, and so forth. The above is a modification of this approach.

The collapsing method selected should be the one that best describes the group and best serves the purposes of the research.

FIGURE 12.1

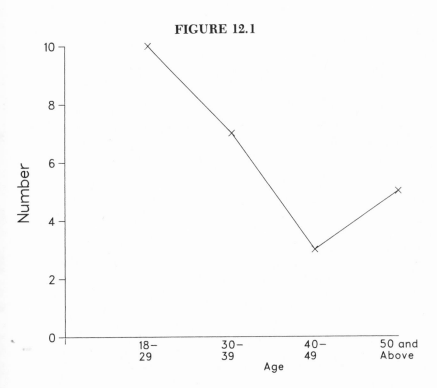

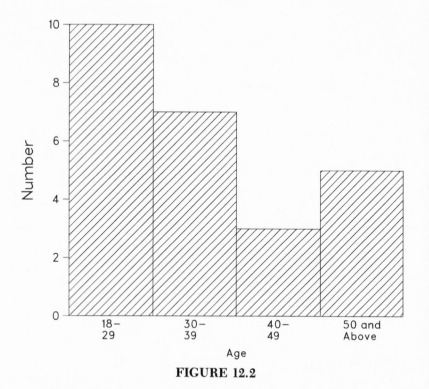

FIGURE 12.2

In collapsing interval variables one must also decide on the number of categories. No hard-and-fast rules can be given for determining this. The fewer the number of categories, the easier it will be to read the distribution. However in collapsing values we lose information, so the more categories we have the more complete the description of the data will be. We must find a compromise between these considerations.

Often it is desirable to display a frequency distribution in the form of a graph such as a line chart or a bar chart or histogram. Figure 12.1 is a line chart of our distribution of ages. Line charts are used only with ordinal or equal interval variables. Figure 12.2 is a bar chart or histogram of the same distribution. The term *histogram* refers to a bar chart of an equal interval variable.

CENTRAL TENDENCY

It is usually desirable to summarize the values for a variable even more than is provided by a frequency distribution. We do this by calculating various measures that characterize the distribution. To begin with, we often want to say where the middle of the distribution is since this allows us to give a single representative value. There are several ways of determining this which are all called measures of central tendency. *Measures of central tendency* include:

1. The *mode*. The mode is the category (value) with the greatest number of cases, the most frequently occurring value. The modal racial-ethnic group in the above data is white. If there is a tie for the category with the largest number of cases then there is no unique modal value. Uncollapsed equal interval variables sometimes have only one case at each value. In that event, we have no mode. We can talk about the mode of collapsed equal interval variables but the way they are collapsed will have a big effect on the determination of the mode. For this reason, the mode is used most often for categorical and ordinal variables and less often for interval data.
2. The *median*. The median is the middle value of the distribution, the point at which half the cases are above and half below. To determine it we have to list the values in order and find the middle one. The median age for our data is thirty-three.
3. The mean is known as the average in ordinary language. The mean is computed by adding up all the values and dividing the sum by the number of cases. The mean age of our subjects is 35.8. The mean is the most widely used measure of central tendency for equal interval variables because many statistical procedures make use of it. A symbolic expression for the mean is

$$\bar{x} = \frac{\Sigma x_i}{n}$$

where $\bar{x}$ represents the mean, x_i represents each value, the capital Greek letter sigma Σ signals to add up all the values, and n represents the number of cases.

The mean may be used only with equal interval variables, the median with ordinal and equal interval variables, and the mode with all three levels of measurement (although ordinal and equal interval variables may need to be collapsed in order to determine a meaningful mode). For equal interval variables either the median or the mean may be the best description of the distribution (the most representative value). The mean has the advantage of making use of all the values, thus it uses more information than does the median. However, it is affected by extreme values and the median is not. If the highest value of a distribution is moved from 10 to 1000, the mean will change while the median will not. For this reason the median is often preferred when extreme values are present.

Suppose we are interested in comparing real estate taxes in two communities of different sizes. In one community there are extreme values; that is, some people pay very large taxes. If we are interested in comparing the relative burden on the taxpayers in the two communities, we might chose to compare median tax payments since the median is a better indication of a typical value in the case of distributions with extreme values. On the other hand, if we are interested in comparing the relative ability of the two communities to provide services (repair streets, provide education, and so forth) it would be better to compare mean tax payments. This is because the ability to provide services depends on the total amount of tax money available to the two communities. Since they have different numbers of people it is necessary to adjust our measure of ability to provide services by dividing the total amount of tax money available by the number of taxpayers. This gives us the mean.

We noted above that interval level techniques may be used with dichotomous variables. We can see that in regard to the mean, as follows. Suppose that our study involves 100 persons. On the dichotomous variable gender we have sixty women and forty men. Thus, the proportion of women is .6. Now code women as 1 and men as 0 and determine the mean of this variable. We will add up sixty 1's and forty 0's for a total of sixty. Divide by 100 to get the mean, .6. Thus the mean of a dichotomous variable with categories coded 1 and 0 is the proportion of cases coded as 1. As a result, a proportion may be interpreted as a mean.

VARIABILITY

A second characteristic of a frequency distribution we often try to summarize is its variability or dispersion, how widely scattered the values are around the middle. We could have two distributions with the same mean: in one the values cluster closely around the mean (little variability), while in the other they are widely scattered (much variability). We need to have numerical measures of much and little variability. The concept of variability is usually applied only to ordinal and equal interval variables. A categorical variable is described by its frequency distribution and modal category.

Range. The range of a variable is the simplest measure of variability: the specification of the highest and lowest values. For equal interval variables the range is often given as the difference between these two values. It is obviously very much affected by extreme values, so its usefulness as a measure of variation is limited.

Interquartile Range. The interquartile range is determined by dividing the group into four equal subgroups (quartiles) and then locating the values at the bottom of the second quartile and the top of the third. For ordinal data the interquartile range is reported as these two values. For equal interval variables it is often given as the difference between these two values. The interquartile range is not affected by a few extreme values because they will lie outside it.

Variance. The variance is a measure used for equal interval variables. It is obtained by subtracting the mean from the value for each case. (Some of these subtractions will result in negative numbers, since some values will be below the mean.) We then square each of the differences (resulting in positive numbers since the square of a negative number is positive) and add them together. Finally we divide by the number of cases to find the variance. The variance might be thought of as the average squared deviation from the mean. All of this is summarized as:

$$\sigma^2 = \frac{\Sigma(x_i - \bar{x})^2}{n}$$

where σ is the lower case Greek letter sigma and σ^2 means the variance. The numerator of this formula is called the *sum of squares* of the variable. The sum of squares plays an important part in advanced statistical analysis.

When we have a sample from a larger population and we want to estimate the population variance from information in the sample, the formula is slightly different. It turns out that in this situation it is better to divide by $n-1$ rather than n so the formula is

$$s^2 = \frac{\Sigma(x_i - \bar{x})^2}{n-1}$$

where s^2 is used instead of σ^2 to represent a sample estimate (sometimes called a *statistic*).

Although the variance is used extensively in statistics, it is difficult to grasp its meaning in concrete terms. The reason for this is that it is an average of squared deviations. Thus the units in which it is expressed are squared units. For example, the variance of the variable age in the above data is 181 square years (using $n-1$ in the denominator). A square year does not have much concrete meaning. For this reason another measure of variability is usually computed: the standard deviation. The *standard deviation* is simply the square root of the variance. It is represented by σ or s depending on whether n or $n-1$ was used in computing the variance. Taking the square root of the variance gets us back to the original units of measurement. The standard deviation of ages in our example is 13.45 years.

Measures of variability are most meaningful when they are used for purposes of comparison. Two or more groups can be compared on the same variable. For example, we might compare two groups in terms of variation in income. In addition, the variation of two variables measured on the same type of scale can be compared within a single group. However, it makes no sense to compare variability of variables that are not measured in the same units. For example, a comparison of variability in age (measured in years) with variability in income (measured in dollars) is meaningless.

If we know the shape of the distribution we can specify what proportion of cases lie within a certain number of standard deviations from the mean. Some texts provide an interpretation of the standard deviation in terms of the normal distribution. In a normal distribution 68 percent of the cases are between plus and minus one standard deviation from the mean and about 95 percent lie within plus or minus two standard deviations. Unfortunately, few naturally occurring distributions are normal in shape.

The normal distribution is most useful in inferential statistics, discussed below.

ASSOCIATION

In the previous section we discussed the description of a single variable at a time (univariate description). Research, however, almost always requires that we pay attention to more than one variable at the same time. For example, the demonstration of a causal relationship between two variables begins by examining the association between the variables.

In associational analysis we usually distinguish between dependent and independent variables. A dependent variable is a variable we want to explain or predict. We think of it as depending on other factors. Sometimes it is called a criterion or response variable. Independent variables are variables we think may affect the dependent variable. Such variables are also called predictor variables.

Crosstabulation. The simplest way to examine association is with crosstabulations, also called crosstabs, crossbreaks, frequency tables, or contingency tables. Crosstabs may be used with any level of measurement, although ordinal and interval variables must be collapsed to a reasonably small number of categories before constructing crosstabs.

A crosstabulation can be found in Table 12.5. We have put the dependent variable in the columns and the independent variable in the rows. Some researchers do it the other way around. The first number in each cell is the number of cases, the second is the percentage that number is of the row total. Computing the percentages allows us to compare groups of unequal size more easily. There are a number of rules for how to calculate percent-

TABLE 12.5   Social Functioning

S.E.S.	High (5–10)	Low (0–4)	Total
High (1–3)	6 (40%)	9 (60%)	15
Low (4–5)	3 (30%)	7 (70%)	10
Total	9	16	25

age tables. Most frequently we compute percents within the categories of the independent variable as in Table 12.5. That is, the total number of cases in each category of the independent variable is used as the denominator for each cell in that row.

We determine whether the two variables in the table are associated or related by comparing the percents within the columns. (If we had figured percents by columns we would compare them across rows.) If they are equal, there is no association. Persons with high socioeconomic status are slightly more likely to be functioning at a high level (we compare 40 percent with 30 percent). The simplest measure of association in a table involving dichotomous variables is the percent difference, here 40% − 30% = 10%. Whether 10 percent indicates a large or a small degree of association depends on the circumstances, the phenomena we are studying, and how it compares with other associations in our study.

When we have variables with more than two categories, determining the nature of the association from the percents is more difficult. Then it is not possible to compute a single percent difference, since more than two percentages need to be compared. Other measures of association are available to use when we have more than two categories. The measures are useful for making comparisons among two or more associations, however, they work best when the variables are either dichotomous or ordered (that is, when both are ordered or dichotomous or one is ordered and the other dichotomous).

Control Variable Analysis. Usually we are interested in the interrelationships among more than two variables. That is, we might be primarily interested in the relationship between variables X and Y, but a third variable Z might intervene in a significant way. For example, the relationship between S.E.S. and social functioning in the above example might be explained by age. This third variable is said to be a control variable.

We explore the effect of the third variable by dividing the group into all of the categories of the third variable and examining the relationship between the two main categories in this context. In our example we would examine the relationship between S.E.S. and social functioning within age categories. The approach is limited when we have a small sample to begin with, since di-

TABLE 12.6   Level of Social Functioning

Unit	High	Low	Total
Experimental	67 (54%)	58	125
Traditional	58 (46%)	67	125
Total	125	125	250

viding a small group into even smaller units will result in too few cases in the subgroups for useful conclusions.

To illustrate these ideas we need to extend our example. Suppose that we are comparing the outcomes of two units in a psychiatric hospital, one a new experimental unit and the other a traditional unit. Our outcome measure is level of social functioning after discharge. This time we are studying 125 former patients from each unit. The results are shown in Table 12.6. From this data it appears that patients from the experimental unit do better slightly more often than those from the traditional unit (whether the 8 percent difference found at high levels of functioning is important could be a matter for argument). However suppose we believe that patients on the experimental unit tended to be from higher socioeconomic classes and that this may explain the result. We decide to control for S.E.S. by looking at the above results for two levels of S.E.S. This is shown in Table 12.7. Now the relationship between type of unit and outcome has practically disappeared. That is, the percent differences in these two tables are only 3 percent.

There are a couple of possible interpretations of an outcome such as this. First, the third variable might be something that occurred before the independent variable and causes differences in both the independent and dependent variables. In that case

TABLE 12.7   Social Functioning

Unit	High	Low	Total
	High S.E.S.		
Experimental	47 63%	28	75
Traditional	30 60%	20	50
Total	77	48	125
	Low S.E.S.		
Experimental	20 40%	30	50
Traditional	28 37%	47	75
Total	48	77	125

the relationship between the dependent and independent variables is said to be *spurious*. Sometimes the third variable is something that occurs between the independent and dependent variables. For example, a job training program might develop self-esteem, which in turn might be related to obtaining a job. In that case, self-esteem would be considered an *intervening* variable, and controlling for it in the same way would result in similar tables. If a relationship disappears when a third variable is controlled, statistical analysis itself cannot determine whether the original relationship was spurious or the third variable is intervening. That decision is based only on the logical ordering of the variables, usually their order of occurrence. It is a good idea to try to draw diagrams of the relationships, as in Figure 12.3.

The original relationship might not disappear when we control for a third variable. It is possible that it will continue to be evident in all of the categories. In such cases we would conclude that the third variable does not play a role in explaining the original relationship. The relationship also may decrease but remain in evidence. In these cases the third variable explains part but not all of the original relationship. On rare occasions the relationship will increase. At such times the third variable is called a *suppressor* variable.

Frequently, however, still another result occurs when a third variable is introduced. In this situation the relationship between the two primary variables changes within the different categories of the control variable. Although this is not a simple finding, it is often an important one. It usually is not possible to summarize the results easily; rather, the primary relationship has to be described for each category of the control variable. The third variable is said to specify the relationship between the first two variables and is called a specifying variable. This is related to the idea of interaction discussed below.

FIGURE 12.3

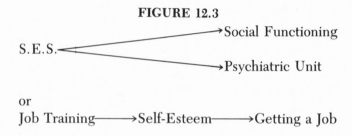

or
Job Training———→Self-Esteem———→Getting a Job

Association Between Equal Interval Variables. Suppose we decide to treat social functioning as an equal interval variable and look at its relationship to the length of hospitalization. When we have two equal interval variables we can graphically display their relationship in a scatterplot that looks like that found in Figure 12.4. Each point on this plot represents one case located in accordance with its values on the two variables. The horizontal line is called the x axis and the vertical line is the y axis. The vertical distance from the x axis indicates level of social functioning (the value of y) while the horizontal distance from the y axis represents length of hospitalization (the value of x). In such plots the vertical axis (y) represents the dependent variable while the horizontal axis (x) represents the independent variable.

If such plots are relatively straight, it is possible to make use of the techniques of linear regression. We begin by assuming that the basic relationship between the two variables can be represented by a straight line, as is Figure 12.5.

FIGURE 12.4

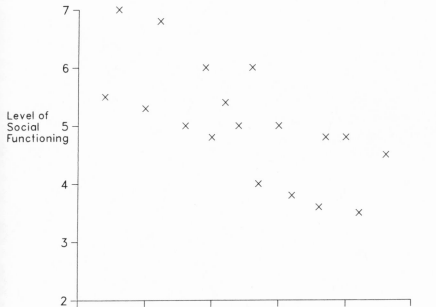

Length of Hospitalization
in Months

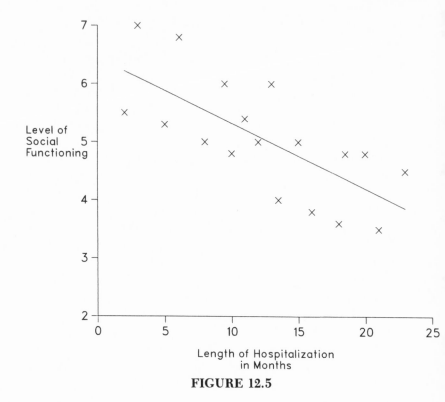

FIGURE 12.5

If all of the points in our scatterplot lie on the straight line, the line would represent the relationship perfectly. In real data this doesn't happen; not all the points will be on the line. The vertical distances between the points and the line indicate the extent to which the line fails to represent the relationship.

Straight lines may be represented algebraically by:

$$y = a + bx$$

where y and x represent variables and a and b are numbers that are known or can be determined. The number a is the intercept of the line, that is, the value of y at which the line crosses the y axis (where $x = 0$). The number b gives the slope of the line, that is, the amount by which y changes for an increase in x of one unit.

For the above line the equation is:

$$y = 6.5 - .125x$$

In this equation the slope is negative, that is, social function-ing decreases on average by .125 units for each increase in hos-pitalization of one month. The relationship is said to be negative or inverse. Of course, relationships can be positive, in which case the line would slope the other way, as in Figure 12.6.

To capture the idea that the above equation is not a perfect representation of the relationship between the two variables, the equation is written:

$$y_i = a + bx_i + e_i$$

where y_i is the value of the dependent variable for any one of the cases (case i), x_i is the value of the independent variable for the same case and e_i represents the vertical distance from the point to the line, sometimes called the *residual* or the *error*. The value e_i may be positive or negative depending on whether the point is above or below the line. This equation is said to be a model for the data. Regression analysis is concerned with determining (or estimating) the values of a and b, (called the *regression coeffi-cients*) and the appropriateness of the model for the data. Deter-

FIGURE 12.6

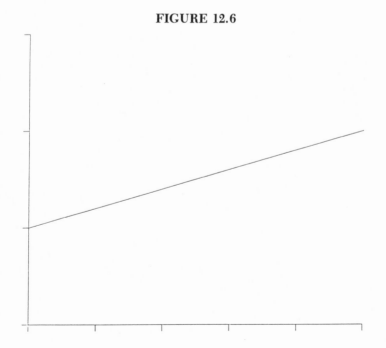

mining how well the data fits includes first, deciding whether or not a linear (straight line) model is appropriate (as opposed to a curved line) and second, measuring how much scatter there is around the line.

The value for b may be found from the data by means of the following formula:

$$b = \frac{\Sigma(x_i - \bar{x})(y_i - \bar{y})}{\Sigma(x_i - \bar{x})^2}$$

The numerator of this formula means that we find the difference between the x value for each case and the x mean, multiply that by the difference between the y value for that case and the y mean and add the results for all cases.

The value for a is determined by:

$$\bar{y} - b\bar{x}$$

Social researchers usually are much more interested in b than in a. The coefficient b indicates the extent to which the dependent variable is affected by the independent variable. If it is large, then a change in x is expected to be accompanied by a large change in y while if b is small, a change in x does not result in much of a change in y. If we want to compare the relationship of x and y in two samples we can compare the two bs. Comparing the relationship of two different independent variables with a dependent variable is problematic, however, because the b coefficients are affected by the variances of the variables. Suppose we are studying the determinants of social functioning and are looking at the effects of income (measured in dollars) and education (measured in years of schooling). We compute two equations like the above, with income and education independent and social functioning dependent. The equations might look like

$$y_i = 3.1 + 0.004I_i + e_i$$

$$y_i = 2.5 + 1.2E_i + e_i$$

Where y means the variable social functioning, I means income, and E means education. This means that a difference of one year of education is accompanied by a difference of 1.2 in social functioning while a difference of one dollar of income is accompanied by a difference of 0.004 in social functioning. From this I am unable to say whether education or income has the greater effect; the b coefficients are not directly comparable, since the units of measurement for education and income are not comparable.

Statisticians get around this problem by computing standardized regression coefficients. Standardized regression coefficients are regression coefficients that have been transformed so that they are comparable.

To get standardized regression coefficients we transform the variables into standard score form before doing our analysis. An individual value is transformed into a standard score by subtracting the mean of the variable and then dividing by the standard deviation. Thus it indicates the number of standard deviations the value is from the mean. The formula is:

$$z_i = \frac{x_i - \bar{x}}{s_x}$$

where z_i is the standard score of value x_i, $\bar{x}$ is the mean and s_x is the standard deviation. For example, in the above equations the standardized coefficients might be:

$$y_i = .4I_i + e_i$$

$$y_i = .6E_i + e_i$$

(When standardized coefficients are computed the intercept term drops out.) Now we can compare the two coefficients and say that education appears to have a larger effect than income.

We cannot determine conclusively a causal relationship between x and y from looking at a regression coefficient. The latter can be large even if there is no causal effect of x on y since other variables may be responsible for the relationship we observe. When we use the term *effect* in statistics we mean that there is a statistical relationship but not necessarily a causal one. Only if we have conducted a well controlled experiment can we presume to have eliminated or controlled the effects of other variables.

Multiple Regression. Regression analysis may be extended to explore the effects of more than one variable at the same time. This is done by including all the variables in the model. For example, the model for two independent variables at once would be:

$$y_i = a + b_1 x_{1i} + b_2 x_{2i} + e_i$$

Estimates of a and the b's can be obtained from the data using formulas similar to those above. However, when we have more than one independent variable we usually use computers to find the coefficients. There are many computer programs available for determining the coefficients so that we do not need to remember the formulas. A model such as this serves a purpose similar to that of dividing a sample into subsamples in crosstabulation analysis. If the relationship between x_1 and y is the same whatever the value of x_2, the b_1 we find can be interpreted as the effect of x_1 on y, holding x_2 constant. Similarly, b_2 can be interpreted as the effect of x_2 on y holding x_1 constant. The analysis of more than one independent variable in this way is called *multiple regression*. Multiple regression can also be used to explore nonlinear relationships between variables. For example, if our scatterplot looked like that in Figure 12.7, a straight line through the collection of points would not represent the relationship adequately, rather we need a curved line like that found in Figure 12.8.

This situation calls for a nonlinear model which might have a term with x squared:

$$y_i = a + b_{11}x_{1i} + b_{12}x_{1i}^2 + e_i$$

FIGURE 12.7

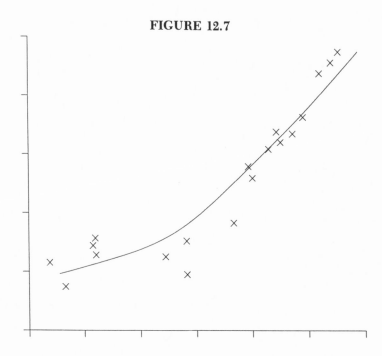

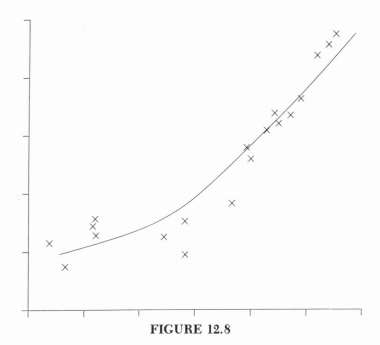

FIGURE 12.8

Sometimes nonlinear regressions require terms with higher powers as well.

Still another use of multiple regression is in examining interactions among variables. An interaction between x_1 and x_2 occurs when the relationship between x_1 and y is different at different levels of x_2. Then the regression model would include a cross-product term, the product of x_1 and x_2:

$$y_i = a + b_1 x_{1i} + b_2 x_{2i} + b_{12} x_{1i} x_{2i} + e_i$$

Prediction. Once we have found the a and the bs we can use them to predict values of y, the dependent variable. We can write prediction equations as:

$$\hat{y}_i = a + b x_i$$

where $\hat{y}_i$ means the predicted value of y for a particular value of x (x_i). The pairs of values x_i, $\hat{y}_i$ represent points that lie on the line $\hat{y}_i = a + b x_i$. We could predict y for a value of x that does not appear in our sample (although the x should be within the range of the x values that do appear). We can also calculate the predicted y values for xs that do appear in our sample. We do that in order to compare the predicted values of y $(\hat{y}_i)$ with the values of y that actually occurred. The difference between these values $(y_i - \hat{y}_i)$ is called the *residual* of y_i (it is an estimate of the e_i above). The residuals will be both positive and negative since the original points lie both above and below the line.

Correlation. We need to have some indication of the strength of our model. If the residuals tend to be small (small in relation to the variation in y), then the independent variables have done a good job in predicting y and our model is relatively good. If on the other hand the residuals tend to be large, the model is not so good. A summary index of the accuracy of prediction is the *correlation coefficient* symbolized by r (in multiple regression it is called the *multiple correlation coefficient* and represented by R). In regression involving only one independent variable, r can range from -1 to $+1$; -1 means the relationship is a perfect negative association (all the cases lie on the regression line so all the residuals are zero) while $+1$ means a perfect positive relationship. An r of zero means there is no relationship (in which case the b coefficient will be zero also and the regression line will be horizontal). In multiple regression, R can range from 0 to $+1$.

The correlation coefficient is determined as follows. The sum of squares of y $(\Sigma(y_i - \bar{y})^2)$ can be thought of as a measure of the amount of variation in y. It can be divided into two parts. The first part is the variation explained by the regression line. It is computed as $\Sigma(\hat{y}_i - \bar{y})^2$. The second part is the unexplained variation of the cases around the line. It is the sum of squares of the residuals $(\Sigma(y_i - \hat{y}_i)^2)$. The square of the correlation coefficient is the ratio of the explained variation to the total variation:

$$r^2 = \frac{\Sigma(\hat{y}_i - \bar{y})^2}{\Sigma(y_i - \bar{y})^2}$$

To find the correlation coefficient we take the square root of this. If we have only one independent variable we attach a plus or minus sign, depending on whether the relationship is positive or negative (this can be determined by the sign of b).

The equation above provides us with the most common interpretation of the correlation coefficient. That is, its square is the proportion of variation of y that is explained by the independent variables.

Regression and correlation analysis is an extensive set of techniques which can be a powerful tool in exploring relationships among equal interval variables.

Inferential Statistics

Up to this point this chapter has been concerned with descriptive statistics, ways of summarizing variables and their relationships. When, as is usually the case, the data are from a sample of a larger population we want to be able to generalize to this level. Inferential statistics is concerned with drawing conclusions about populations from samples.

Suppose we find a relationship between two variables in a sample. Can it be asserted that there is also a relationship between these variables in the population from which the sample was drawn? Does the study sample actually represent the population? How can it be determined that the responses obtained from the sample actually reflect the responses of the population? There are no fully satisfying answers to these questions. In fact much of the discipline of statistics is devoted to finding ways to deal with them.

Inferential statistics may be used to draw conclusions about populations when the sample is drawn probabilistically. The simplest kind of probability sample is the simple random sample. In a simple random sample all members of the population have the same probability of being in the sample and the sample members are selected using some kind of random procedure, such as a table of random numbers. When we have a probability sample we can draw conclusions about the population, but those conclusions will be probabilistic (they will not be true definitely but will have probabilities attached to them). We are able to compute these probabilities.

There are two basic procedures in inferential statistics: confidence interval construction and hypothesis testing. They have the same mathematical bases and are closely related.

CONFIDENCE INTERVAL CONSTRUCTION

In the above example of a study of former psychiatric patients we found that the mean age was 35.8. If our group was sampled from a larger population it is likely that the population mean would not be exactly 35.8. However if the sample was random, we would be able to specify an interval within which we expect the population mean to lie. More formally, we can construct sentences like: There is a .95 (95 percent) probability that the population mean lies between *a* and *b*. The numbers *a* and *b* can be calculated. We cannot be absolutely sure the population mean is between *a* and *b*; rather we will have 95 percent confidence. Of course we could make the probability larger (for instance, .99) or smaller (for instance, .90). If we make the probability larger, the confidence interval will be larger and vice versa.

Confidence intervals can be constructed for all sorts of population characteristics (called population *parameters*), for example, proportions, differences in proportions in two groups, differences in means of two groups, correlation coefficients, and regression coefficients.

HYPOTHESIS TESTING

Hypothesis testing or significance testing begins by establishing a hypothesis about the situation in the population. This hypothesis, called an *alternative hypothesis*, specifies that the two variables are believed to be associated. There are several ways to say this. We may state that there is an association between the two variables or that persons with longer hospitalizations are likely to be functioning at a lower level. The first of these hypotheses is called a *nondirectional* or *two-tailed* hypothesis, while the second is called a *directional* or *one-tailed* hypothesis. A directional hypothesis specifies how the two variables are related while a nondirectional hypothesis states that there is an association but does not specify the nature of it.

It is possible that our sample might show some association between the variables (that is, it might look like the alternative hypothesis is true) while there is no association in the population. At this point, a contorted logic begins. We cannot actually test the alternative hypothesis; rather we test another hypothesis called the *null hypothesis*. The null hypothesis, which states that there is no association between the variables, is the logical opposite of the alternative hypothesis. We then determine its probable truth or falsity. If it is likely that the null hypothesis is false, then we will accept the alternative. For our example, the null hypothesis would be: There is no relationship between length of hospitalization and level of functioning.

The process of hypothesis testing involves calculating the probability that we would have obtained a sample with this much association if the null hypothesis is true. This is done by first calculating a *test statistic* the probability of which can be determined by looking at tables in statistics books. (Alternatively, computers have been programmed to compute the probability of test statistics.) Various test statistics are used with differing levels of measurement. Some of the test statistics used in social research are shown in Table 12.8.

If we find the probability is low (.05 or lower), it is unlikely that our sample results would have occurred if the null hypothesis is true. Hence, we accept the alternative. We say then that the result is statistically significant at the probability level we calculated.

SAMPLE SIZE

In general, the larger the sample, the greater the chance of rejecting the null hypothesis if in fact it is false. The probability

TABLE 12.8

Level of Measurement	Null Hypothesis	Test Statistic
Two categorical variables	Difference in percentages is zero	Chi-square (χ^2)
One categorical and one interval variable	Difference in means is zero	*t*-test
One categorical (many categories) and one interval variable	No differences in means	F (analysis of variance)
Two interval variables	Correlation coefficient is zero	F (analysis of variance of regression)

of rejecting the null hypothesis if it is false is called the power of the statistical test. The larger the sample size, the greater the power. In fact, with a very large sample it is likely that the null hypothesis will be rejected even if the association in the population is very small.

It is important to keep separate the ideas of association and significance or hypothesis testing. It is possible for a very small association to be statistically significant. This result would tend to occur most often in large samples. It is also possible for the reverse to occur—a large association proving insignificant—with a small sample.

THE CHI SQUARE TEST

The chi square (χ^2) test is used to determine whether it is likely that two categorical or ordinal variables are associated. It may be used with equal interval variables if these are collapsed to categories before the analysis is performed. We begin with a crosstabulation of the two variables as in Table 12.9.

Even if there were no association between the variables in the population, it is possible to take a random sample with this much association between the variables (a difference of 10 percent). We would want to estimate the probability of this occurrence. The computation of χ^2 begins with the determination of the expected counts in each cell of the table. The expected counts are the numbers in each cell that we would expect, on the average, if the null hypothesis were true. The expected count for a cell is computed by multiplying the total number of cases in that cell's row by the column total, then dividing by the total number of cases in the table. For example, to find the expected count in the upper left hand corner of the above table we multiply 15 by 9 and

TABLE 12.9   Social Functioning

S.E.S.	High (5–10)	Low (0–4)	Total
High (1–3)	6 (40%)	9 (60%)	15
Low (4–5)	3 (30%)	7 (70%)	10
Total	9	16	25

divide by 25. The result is 5.4. Expected counts are usually not whole numbers.

Then χ^2 is computed by subtracting the expected count from the observed count in each cell, squaring that number and dividing by the expected count. These values are then added up for all the cells. The procedure may be summarized by the formula:

$$\chi^2 = \Sigma[(O-E)/E]^2$$

where the capital Greek letter sigma (Σ) indicates the addition of what follows for all cells. For our example the χ^2 is .053.

The computed χ^2 is then looked up in a table (called a table of the χ^2 distribution) found in most statistics books. To use the table it is necessary to determine the degrees of freedom for the computed χ^2. The degrees of freedom are found by subtracting one from the number of rows and one from the number of columns and multiplying these numbers together. This is expressed mathematically by $(r-1)(c-1)$. For the table above the degrees of freedom are $(2-1)(2-1) = 1$. To use the χ^2 table we find the line for our degrees of freedom and determine the largest entry in that line which is smaller than our computed χ^2. We look at the probability listed at the top of that column. That number is the probability that we would have gotten our sample results if the null hypothesis is true. If the probability is small (for example, .05 or .01), we reject the null hypothesis and accept the alternative that there is some association between our variables. If no entry in the appropriate line is smaller than our computed χ^2 we must accept the null hypothesis. In our example the χ^2 value is smaller than any of the table values for one degree of freedom so we conclude that the data does not give us sufficient grounds to claim there is a relationship between S.E.S. and social functioning in the population.

THE T-TEST

The *t*-test is used to test the null hypothesis that the means of a variable in two populations are the same. The variable must have equal intervals. The test might be used in an experiment in which we compare an experimental group with a control group on some equal interval outcome measure. The null hypothesis would be that the experiment had no effect or that the two groups would have about the same average outcomes. Again, it is possible that we would have gotten some difference if there were no differences in the population means.

As in the chi square, the t-test requires the computation of a statistic (the t) which is then looked up in a table. The computation of the t requires a number of steps:

1. Find the difference between the sample means. This can be symbolized as: $\bar{x}_1 - \bar{x}_2$.
2. Find the sum of squares for each group. This is done by subtracting from the value for each case the mean of that group, squaring the difference, and then adding these numbers together for the entire group. This is symbolized by $\Sigma(x_{1i} - \bar{x}_1)^2$ and $\Sigma(x_{2i} - \bar{x}_2)^2$ where x_{1i} is a case in the first group, x_{2i} a case in the second group, and the Σs mean add together for all cases in the group.
3. Pool these sums of squares. That is, add them together.
4. Divide this number by the degrees of freedom, the sum of the numbers of cases in each group minus two $(n_1 + n_2 - 2)$. This is symbolized as:

$$s^2 = \frac{\Sigma(x_{1i} - \bar{x}_1)^2 + \Sigma(x_{2i} - \bar{x}_2)^2}{n_1 + n_2 - 2}$$

This gives a pooled estimate of the variance of the scores within each population.

5. Divide this variance estimate by each of the sample sizes and add these numbers: $s^2/n_1 + s^2/n_2$
6. Take the square root of this number: $s_{1-2} = \sqrt{(s^2/n_1 + s^2/n_2)}$

This gives the standard error of the difference in sample means. A *standard error* is an estimated standard deviation. Imagine taking a very large number of pairs of samples from our populations, each sample the same size as the ones we actually did take. For each pair we compute (still only in imagination) the difference between sample means. Imagine now a list (a very long list) of these differences. The standard error is an estimate of what the standard deviation of these differences would be. It turns out that we can make an estimate of this standard deviation without actually taking a lot of samples; in fact, we make the estimate using only the one pair of samples we have.

7. Divide the result from step one $(\bar{x}_1 - \bar{x}_2)$ by the result from step 6. This is the computed t statistic.

The t statistic is looked up in a table similar to the χ^2 table. The degrees of freedom for it is $n_1 + n_2 - 2$. The interpretation is similar to that described above for χ^2. If the calculated value is greater than the table value for a particular probability, then there is less than that probability that we would have gotten this much difference in our sample means if the null hypothesis is true.

ANALYSIS OF VARIANCE

The analysis of variance (abbreviated ANOVA) is a very extensive set of powerful techniques for the analysis of equal interval data. We will consider here only the simplest kind, the one-way analysis of variance. One-way ANOVA is an extension of the t-test to the situation in which we have more than two groups and an equal interval outcome variable. For example, we might want to compare several states in terms of the average length of stay of children in foster care. The null hypothesis is that the means of the groups (states) are all equal. The data from samples of children is arranged in a table like this:

State				
A	B	C	D	E

In each column of this table we list the lengths of stay of children in a sample from that state.

The analysis of variance proceeds by dividing up the total variation of the equal interval dependent variable into two parts, the within groups variation and the between groups variation. We do this by dividing up the total sum of squares. The within groups variation is found in the same way as in the t-test; that is, we calculate the sum of squares within each group and then add these together for all groups. This may be symbolized as follows: $s.s._{\cdot w} = \Sigma\Sigma(x_{ij} - \bar{x}_{i\cdot})^2$. In this formula $s.s._{\cdot w}$ means the sum of squares within groups, $\bar{x}_{i\cdot}$ is the mean of the ith group, and x_{ij} is one value (the jth value) in the ith group. The second summation sign (the second Σ) in the formula tells us to compute the sum of squares in each group (the sum of the squared deviations of values from their mean) and the first Σ tells us to add all of these group sums of squares together.

The between groups sum of squares is found by subtracting from the mean of each group the mean of all of the cases taken together (without reference to group membership; this is called the *grand mean*). We then square that difference, multiply by the number of cases in that group and add this together for all groups. This is mathematically expressed by

$$s.s._b = \Sigma n_i (\bar{x}_i. - \bar{x}..)^2$$

where $s.s._b$ means the sum of squares between groups, n_i is the number of cases in the ith group, $\bar{x}..$ is the grand mean and all other symbols have the same meaning as above.

The sum of squares within and the sum of squares between add up to the total sum of squares; that is, the sum of squares that is found if we subtract the grand mean from each individual value, square that difference and add these squared differences for all cases. This is written:

$$\Sigma\Sigma(x_{ij} - \bar{x}..)^2 = \Sigma\Sigma(x_{ij} - \bar{x}_i.)^2 + \Sigma n_i(\bar{x}_i. - \bar{x}..)^2$$

We now find the within groups mean square and the between groups mean square. The mean squares are found by dividing the sums of squares by their degrees of freedom. The degrees of freedom for between groups is $k-1$ and for within groups $N-k$, where N is the total number of cases in the analysis.

All of this can be summarized as in Table 12.10. The last column of Table 12.10 contains the F statistic (also called the F ratio). The F statistic is found by dividing the mean square between by the mean square within. The test of the null hypothesis that all the group means are equal is made by looking up the calculated F statistic in a table of Fs. The F statistic has associated with it two degrees of freedom, one for its numerator $(k-1)$ and the other for its denominator $(N-k)$. Suppose the calculated F statis-

TABLE 12.10

Source	S.S.	d.f.	M.S.	F
Between	$\Sigma n_i(\bar{x}_i. - \bar{x}..)^2$	$k-1$	$s.s._b/(k-1)$	$m.s._b/m.s._w$
Within	$\Sigma\Sigma(x_{ij} - \bar{x}_i.)^2$	$N-k$	$s.s._w/(N-k)$	
Total	$\Sigma\Sigma(x_{ij} - \bar{x}..)^2$	$N-1$		

tic exceeds the table value for our particular degrees of freedom and for some probability, for instance .05. We would conclude that if the null hypothesis is true, the probability of getting our sample means is less than .05. Since this is a relatively small probability and since we actually got these sample means we would conclude that it is unlikely than the null hypothesis is true. Under some circumstances, we might want to be very, very confident of our conclusions. Then we would insist that the probability be even lower (.01 or even .001) before we reject the null hypothesis and accept the alternative.

ANALYSIS OF VARIANCE OF REGRESSION

The ideas of the analysis of variance can be used in regression analysis to further our understanding of relationships between equal interval variables. First, we locate the regression line (that is, we compute the a and b). Focusing on the dependent variable, we can think of the deviation of the value of each case from the mean as composed of two parts, the distance of that value from the regression line and the distance of the regression line from the mean. For the ith case we may symbolize this as follows:

$$(y_i - \bar{y}) = (y_i - \hat{y}_i) + (\hat{y}_i - \bar{y})$$

where $\hat{y}_i$ lies on the regression line.

This represents matters in terms of a single case. We can summarize things for all cases by squaring each side of the above equation and adding together all cases. When that is done it turns out that the following equation is true:

$$\Sigma(y_i - \bar{y})^2 = \Sigma(y_i - \hat{y}_i)^2 + \Sigma(\hat{y}_i - \bar{y})^2$$

The left side of this equation is the total sum of squares for the dependent variable y. The right side of the equation shows how the total sum of squares can be divided into two parts. The first part $(\Sigma(y_i - \hat{y}_i)^2)$ reflects the scatter of the points representing the cases around the regression line. As stated previously, we call this the residual or error sum of squares. The second part reflects the portion of the variation in y that we are able to account for by x. It is called the regression sum of squares. Two mean squares are formed by dividing by certain degrees of freedom.

The degrees of freedom for regression is q, the number of independent variables (only one in the above example). The degrees of freedom for residual is $N - q - 1$ where N is the total number of cases. All of this can be summarized as in Table 12.11.

TABLE 12.11

Source	S.S.	d.f.	M.S.	F
Regression	$\Sigma(\hat{y}_i - \bar{y})^2$	q	$S.S._{\cdot reg}/q$	$m.s._{\cdot reg}/m.s._{\cdot res}$
Residual	$\Sigma(y_i - \hat{y}_i)^2$	$N - q - 1$	$S.S._{\cdot res}/(N - q - 1)$	
Total	$\Sigma(y_i - \bar{y})^2$	$N - 1$		

As indicated in the last column of Table 12.11 an F statistic is calculated as the ratio of the mean square for regression divided by the mean square for residual. The F has q and $N - q - 1$ degrees of freedom. It is used to test the null hypothesis that there is no relationship in the population between any of the independent variables and the dependent variable. Equivalently, it tests the null hypothesis that all the regression coefficients (except a) are zero.

Finally, as indicated above, the square of the correlation coefficient r (or the square of the multiple correlation coefficient R) is equal to the ratio of the regression sum of squares to the total sum of squares.

Computers

In recent years computers have pervaded everyday life. They have been used in the analysis of data from social science research for many years. It is therefore, useful to know something about what they can do and how they work.

Computers are electronic machines that perform arithmetic and logical operations. By arithmetic operations we mean simply addition, subtraction, multiplication, and division. The power of computers is due to two things:

1. They can perform very long and complex chains of operations very quickly. Some computers are able to add two numbers in a millionth of a second.
2. Computers can perform logical operations. They are able to decide whether something is true or false, for example,

whether or not a variable value is equal to zero. A computer can be instructed to do one thing if it is false and another if it is true.

Computers are operated by giving them a series of instructions about the operations they are to perform. The set of instructions is called a *program*.

During the early years of the computer revolution, computer engineers were concerned with developing ever bigger and more powerful machines (sometimes called main frame computers). Such machines are very expensive and thus are available only in large organizations like businesses or universities. Recently, mini- and microcomputers have been developed. These smaller and less expensive machines are becoming affordable by individuals and small organizations like social agencies. The smaller machines have been made possible by the extraordinary miniaturization of electronic components enabling thousands of transistors (electronic switches found in computers) and other elements to be placed on tiny chips.

Main frame computers are usually operated in a time-sharing manner. That is, it is possible for many people to use a machine at virtually the same time. Computers are used in one of two modes: (1) interactive or conversational mode and (2) batch mode. In the interactive or conversational mode the user talks with the computer, asking questions or giving instructions to which the computer responds almost immediately. In batch mode a series of instructions (a *program*) is submitted to the computer. The instructions are carried out at some later time (sometimes only a few seconds later) producing an *output*, a printed record of the results.

At one time, instructions and data were given to computers by way of punched cards. Although that method still is used occasionally for batch jobs, today users usually communicate with computers through terminals. *Terminals* are devices with typewriter-like keyboards (for entering instructions or data) and either a screen or a printing mechanism which displays the user's instructions and the computer's responses.

The process of analyzing data on a computer involves three main steps: (1) data entry, (2) data editing, and (3) the actual analysis. Data entry is the process of giving the computer the data, that is, the values of the variables for each of the cases. This usually is done through punched cards or a terminal. The data is stored in machine readable form on a magnetic disk or on magnetic tape. Since errors might have been made in coding the data or in entering it into the machine, the computer can be used to help edit (a process called cleaning the data). Finally, the computer is used to perform the actual analysis.

As noted above, a computer operates on the basis of a set of instructions or programs. Actually computers use a whole set of programs at one time, arranged in a hierarchy. These are written in various languages. The hardware (the electronic components) in a computer responds only to instructions in the form of strings of zeros and ones called *machine language*. This is very difficult for people to read or write, so there is another language that contains elementary commands in the form of strings of letters. This is called *assembly language*. A program known as an *assembler* translates assembly language into machine language. Next up the hierarchy are languages that contain more complex instructions; these are what are usually referred to as computer languages. There are a large number of computer languages, each differing somewhat in their purposes. Examples are Fortran (for FORmula TRANslation), Cobol, Algol, and Basic. Programs that translate these languages into assembly language (which is in turn translated into machine language) are called *compilers*. A computer programmer knows one or more computer languages but may know very little about assembly language or machine language.

Finally, there are large and complex systems or packages of programs. A system is a set of general purpose programs written in one of the computer languages. Systems are written in such a way as to permit their use in a variety of specific situations. For example, a system may be told to construct frequency distributions and crosstabulations and compute a series of correlations on a set of data. There are a number of systems that have been developed for statistical analysis including the Statistical Package for the Social Sciences (SPSS), SCSS (the conversational version of SPSS), BMDP (Biomedical Computer Programs), the Statistical Analysis System (SAS), and Interactive Data Analysis (IDA). The researcher communicates with a system using English words. It is, however, necessary to know the words to which a system responds. Today, researchers often know little about computer programming itself, relying instead on statistical systems.

Computers also have a set of programs called the *operating system* (OS for short). The operating system coordinates the activities of various parts of the computer and schedules the work of the many people who may be using the machine at any one time.

PARTS OF A COMPUTER

Figure 12.9 is a simplified diagram of a mainframe or minicomputer.

The central processing unit (CPU) is the core of the computer. It is the part that actually does the work and coordinates the other parts.

The core memory is a set of electronic switches in which data and instructions are stored (in the form of chains of zeros and ones) for very fast access by the CPU.

The other parts of the diagram are called input-output (I-O) devices.

Disk memory consists of a series of disks something like phonograph records. Instead of grooves, the disks are covered with a magnetic material on which information can be stored. Retrieval of data from disks takes a little longer than from core memory.

Reels of tape can be mounted on magnetic tape machines for the storage of data and programs. Magnetic tape is an economical way to store data but retrieval of information takes longer and is more cumbersome than from disk memory.

High speed printers turn out a whole line at a time (they are

FIGURE 12.9

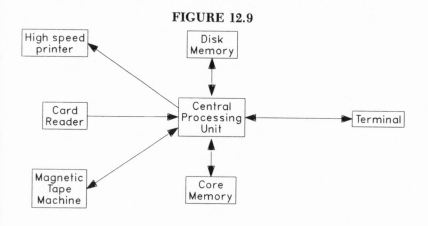

sometimes called line printers) and therefore can produce large amounts of output very quickly.

A card reader reads decks of punched cards (commonly known as I.B.M. cards) and sends the information on them to the computer.

The diagram of a desk top microcomputer would look very similar. Usually terminals are not connected to them (although they can be), so the keyboard, screen, CPU, and core memory may all be in the same cabinet. Microcomputers use *floppy disk* units which are much smaller instead of rigid disks. Tape machines, card readers, and printers can be attached to microcomputers.

STEPS IN USING COMPUTERS FOR DATA ANALYSIS

In this section we give an example of how the most popular social science computer system is used to set up a data file, store it in disk memory, and then retrieve the file for statistical manipulations. The example will involve using SPSS in batch mode. This brief discussion cannot substitute for study of the SPSS manual. We will write an SPSS program which will be carried out by the computer at some point after we submit it. However, we will write the program interactively; that is, we will type in the program instructions at a terminal. As we do so, the computer will store the instructions (it keeps them in core memory), but will not carry them out until we tell it to do so. Since we will probably make mistakes as we are typing, we will correct those mistakes before submitting the job. This storing and correcting of the program will be done using a text editor program. An example of a text editing program is Superwylbur.

To use a big computer we usually need to have an account with the computer. Assuming we have an account, we find a terminal, turn it on, and begin by logging on to the computer; that is, we must get the terminal and the computer connected with each other. The process of logging on varies from place to place, but typically it involves giving the computer an account number and a password known only to you and the machine. You may also need to tell the computer what kind of terminal you are using.

Next we tell the machine we want to use the text editor and we proceed to type in the program. A program to set up a file of the data in Table 12.1 might look like this:

```
/ /SETUP JOB (2LA189, JRS),SCHUER,RE = 260K
/ /  EXEC SPSS,
/ /  OUTFILE = '$2LA189.JRS.DATA',OUTVOL = STOR09
DATA LIST          FIXED(1)/1 CASE 1-2 RACE 4 AGE 6-7 SOCFUNC 9
                   SES 11
INPUT MEDIUM       CARD
N OF CASES         25
VAR LABELS         CASE CASE NUMBER/
                   SOCFUNC LEVEL OF FUNCTIONING/
                   SES SOCIO-ECONOMIC STATUS
VALUE LABELS       RACE (1)WHITE (2)BLACK (3)HISPANIC
FREQUENCIES        GENERAL = RACE TO SES
READ INPUT DATA
01  1  32  7  1
[24 more lines of data]
SAVE FILE          DATA
```

The first three lines of this program are instructions to the operating system of the computer. The information on these lines depends on the particular computer and the way it is programmed at the particular institution. The lines above are those I would use at the University of Chicago. They are IBM job control language. The first line is the job line. It gives the job a name (SETUP), provides the computer our account number (2LA189.JRS) and the programmer name (SCHUER), and tells how much core memory we will need for the job (260K). The second line calls the SPSS program. The third line tells the computer that once we have constructed a data file it is to be stored on disk. The name of the file will be $2LA189.JRS.DATA and it will be stored on a disk unit named STOR09.

The rest of the lines are instructions to the SPSS program. The words starting in the first column of these lines are called the *control field*. They tell SPSS what kind of instruction the line is. The words starting in column 16 are called the *specification field*. They give the actual instructions.

The DATA LIST line names the variables and tells where on the data lines (to follow) the variables are to be found. Fixed/(1) identifies how the values are typed on the data lines (fixed format) and indicates that there is one line of data for each case. CASE

1-2 means that the first variable is named CASE and the values are found in columns 1 and 2 of each data line. The names and locations of the other variables follow. The next line is a continuation line. There was not enough room on the DATA LIST line to list all of the variables so the list continues on the next line. The control field (columns 1-16) of continuation lines is left blank.

The next line (INPUT MEDIUM) identifies where the data are to be read from (for example, from disk or tape). Card means the data are contained later in this program. The use of the term card is a throwback to the days when programs were punched on computer cards.

The N OF CASES line informs SPSS that we have twenty-five cases. The VAR LABELS lines (including two continuation lines) gives some of our variables labels which are more informative than the variable names. Variable names cannot be more than eight letters long and can have no blanks in them. Variable labels will be printed on the output. Value labels serve the same purpose for values of variables.

The FREQUENCIES line asks for frequency distributions to be printed for some of our variables. READ INPUT DATA indicates that the data lines come next. Finally, the SAVE FILE line requests that the file of data, variable names, and labels be kept on disk memory.

The program as printed above has no errors in it (I hope). When we type it in, however, we will probably make mistakes. We will give instructions to the text editing program to correct these errors (the nature of these instructions depends on the text editing program). Once we think we have the program right we will ask to have it stored in disk memory (in case there are errors we haven't caught or in case we want to use it again at some point). Then we will tell the computer to actually run the program, that is, to perform the instructions.

After the program has run and if there are no errors in it, we will get a printout of the frequencies for our variables. We will also have a file of our data stored on disk. The names and labels of the variables and values will also be stored. If at a later point we want to do more statistical analysis with our data, we will need only to write a program to get the data and perform the analysis. This is an example:

```
/ /ANALYSIS JOB (2LA189, JRS),SCHUER,RE = 260K
/ /  EXEC SPSS,
/ /  INFILE = '$2LA189.JRS.DATA',INVOL = STOR09
GET FILE        DATA
CROSSTABS       TABLES = SES BY SOCFUNC
OPTIONS         4,5
STATISTICS      1
PEARSON CORR    AGE,SOCFUNC,SES
STATISTICS      1
```

In spite of our efforts to correct errors, some may remain at the time we run the program. If so, SPSS will not be able to do what we wanted it to do, but it will detect our errors and print messages telling us about them. We can then retrieve our stored program, correct the errors, and resubmit the program. Some computers allow you to read the output at the terminal before it is actually printed, thus saving time in detecting and correcting errors.

OTHER USES OF COMPUTERS

Besides their use in data analysis, computers can be used by human service professionals for other things as well. Some of these other uses are:

1. *The maintenance and retrieval of records.* Case material can be entered into the computer and single cases or groups of cases can be retrieved quickly. Thus the computer can partially replace filing systems.
2. *Text editing.* Material such as reports can be typed into a computer and then edited, that is, corrected or revised. Revision does not require retyping the entire document. The revised version can then be printed out by the computer. This book was written and edited on a computer. In fact, a computer even checked the spelling and helped to set the type.
3. *Financial accounting.* Computers can keep the books and help executives manage agencies.
4. *Simulation.* For example, an agency executive can construct a model of his agency and then use a computer to predict what would happen if certain things were done. Another example is

the simulation of intervention processes. That is, it is possible to use the computer to predict what will happen if one does such and such in a particular situation.

Summary

As indicated at the beginning of this chapter, statistical analysis is a large area which can be summarized only briefly in a book such as this. It can be divided into two broad areas: description and inference. In turn, descriptive statistics can be divided into univariate statistics (the analysis of a single variable at a time) and associational statistics, concerned with the relationships among variables. Univariate statistics includes frequency distributions, measures of central tendancy (the mean, median, and mode) and measures of variability (the range, interquartile range, variance, and standard deviation). Associational analysis involves the use of crosstabulations and, for equal interval variables, correlation and regression.

Inferential statistics is concerned with drawing conclusions about populations from samples. Ideally, such samples should be selected randomly from their populations. The two major inferential techniques are confidence interval construction and hypothesis testing.

The chapter concludes with a section on the use of computers in data analysis.

Bibliography

A few elementary texts in statistics are:

Hubert M. Blalock, *Social Statistics*, rev. 2d ed, New York: McGraw Hill, 1979.

James Davis, *Elementary Survey Analysis*, Englewood Cliffs, N. J.: Prentice-Hall, 1971.

Morris Rosenberg, *The Logic of Survey Analysis*, New York: Basic Books, 1968.

Sidney Siegel, *Non-Parametric Statistics for the Behavioral Sciences*, New York: McGraw Hill, 1956.

Robert S. Weiss, *Statistics in Social Research*, New York: John Wiley and Sons, 1968.

Statistical system manuals include:

BMDP, Biomedical Computer Programs: P Series, Berkeley, Cal.: University of California Press, 1979.

Statistical Package for the Social Sciences, 2d ed., New York: McGraw Hill, 1975.

SPSS Update 7-9, New York: McGraw Hill, 1981.

SCSS A User's Guide to the SCSS Conversational System, New York: McGraw Hill, 1980.

SPSS Primer, New York: McGraw Hill, 1975.

SAS User's Guide, Raleigh, N. C.: SAS Institute, 1982.

User's Manual for IDA, New York: McGraw Hill, 1980.

Index